G000253873

CAR

THE EVOLUTION OF THE AUTOMOBILE

Cover memorabilia captions, clockwise from top left:

- "Safety Fast!" was the slogan that the MG Car Company
  adopted in the late 1930s and continued to use well beyond
  1953, when the MG TF pictured on the poster first appeared (p.75).
- The 1930 Monte Carlo Rally poster, painted by French artist
  and illustrator Robert Falcucci (p.45).
- 1934 advert for Peugeot featuring the 401 (p.51).
- Drawing from Jaguar's archives of a Series 1 E-Type (p.119).
- Charles Stewart Rolls during the 1901 Paris-Berlin race driving a
  French Mors car (p.15).
- Detailed cutaway shows the BRM P57 Formula 1 car in which
  Graham Hill became World Champion in 1962 (p.137).
- Hans Liska's image of Karl Kling's Mercedes-Benz type W196
  R in the 1954 French Grand Prix at Reims (p.84).
- The 1895 Duryea Patent (p.13).
- Alfa Romeo Giulietta design drawings (p.77).
- Annotated blueprint of a Peugeot Chassis from Swiss engineer Georges
  Henry Roesch's notebook (pp.22–3).
- The 1886 patent document for Benz & Co (p.11).

THIS IS AN ANDRÉ DEUTSCH BOOK

This edition published in 2015 by André Deutsch
A division of the Carlton Publishing Group
20 Mortimer Street
London
W1T 3JW

First published in 2012

Text © Carlton Books Limited 2012
Design © Carlton Books Limited 2012, 2015

This book is sold subject to the condition that it shall not, by way of trade
or otherwise, be lent, resold, hired out or otherwise circulated without the
publisher's prior written consent in any form of cover or binding other than
that in which it is published and without a similar condition including the
condition, being imposed upon the subsequent purchaser.

All rights reserved

Printed in China

A CIP catalogue for this book is available from the British Library

ISBN: 978 0 23300 460 0

CAR

THE EVOLUTION OF THE AUTOMOBILE

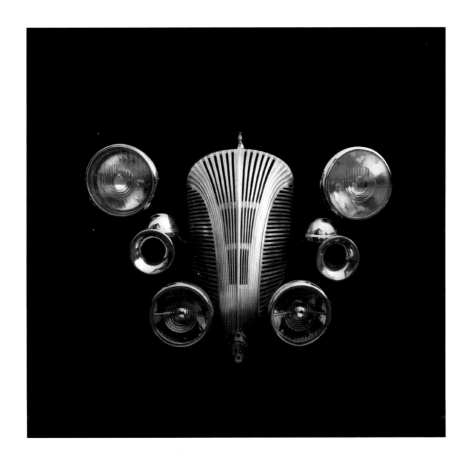

ROD GREEN

ANDRE
DEUTSCH

Contents

Horseless Carriages

The automobile in the twenty-first century is an indispensable part of everyday life for countless millions all over the world. Many people think of their cars as almost part of their family. Yet it was not always this way. In the early days of the car, it was seen as a noisy nuisance – an experimental plaything for eccentric inventors and wealthy aristocrats. This was not entirely true. Early automobiles were very much at the forefront of industrial engineering development.

The story of the car begins with the appearance of the famous Benz Patent Motorwagen in 1885 … or does it? Karl Benz (see box feature page 11) is often regarded as the father of the automobile, but there had been many attempts to produce "horseless carriages" before Benz came along. Various designs for wind-powered vehicles, such as windmills on wheels, date back to the fourteenth century

and a steam-powered toy car is said to have been made for the Chinese Kangxi Emperor (ruled 1661–1722) by a Belgian missionary in 1672. The first true steam-powered vehicle was probably the *fardier à vapeur* built in 1769 by French inventor Nicholas-Joseph Cugnot (1725–1804). Intended to pull heavy cannon, Cugnot's vehicle was a cumbersome beast, as were most of the early steam efforts. The problem was that the steam engine had to be a bit of a monster. Building a

ABOVE Trevithick's London Steam Carriage carried eight passengers for 16.5 km (10 miles) through London's streets in 1803, with the roads closed to other traffic. It was expensive to run, however, and was eventually scrapped.

OPPOSITE Cugnot's steam-powered tricycle was intended for military use over rough terrain but it had poor weight distribution, making it difficult to control.

small steam engine that would produce the same sort of power as a large engine meant using higher steam pressure, and many feared that a high-pressure steam engine would blow itself apart. The rough roads of the time, coupled with inadequate suspension and wooden wheels with iron tyres (rubber tyres did not appear until the middle of the nineteenth century), caused jolting and vibration that threatened to shake the machinery to pieces and even made it difficult to keep the boiler alight. Nevertheless, the motoring pioneers steamed ahead with Oliver Evans (1755–1819) taking out the first US patent for a steam car in 1789 and Cornishman Richard Trevithick (1771–1833) running his London Steam Carriage through the streets of the capital in 1803.

The development of steam coaches and carriages continued throughout the nineteenth century, but the introduction of the steam locomotive and the expansion of the rail networks clearly demonstrated that the best place for the heavy steam engines on land was on flat, smooth rails. At sea, steam power really

came into its own and, just as it dominated the railways, steam power was to rule the waves for the next hundred years.

Back on the roads, there was increasing interest in a different kind of horseless carriage that was quieter, lighter, cleaner and seemed to be far less dangerous than the steam car. In the 1830s, Scotsman Robert Anderson (dates unknown) invented a rudimentary electric carriage, although it wasn't until 1881, when Frenchman Camille Faure (1840–1898) improved upon the rechargeable lead acid battery his fellow Frenchman Gaston Planté (1834–1889) had made, that electric cars really began to make sense. Britain and France led the development of electric vehicles, but by 1897 the Electric Carriage and Wagon Company of Philadelphia had supplied a fleet of electric New York taxis. Within two years, electric cars were selling in greater numbers in America than any other type and in 1899 a Belgian electric racing car called *Le Jamais Contente* set a world land-speed record of 106 kmph (66 mph).

By then, however, the internal combustion engine was moving into the fast lane. Unlike a steam engine, where the fuel is burned outside the engine (external combustion), the internal combustion engine burns its fuel inside a cylinder. The explosion this creates pushes a piston and this movement is eventually used to turn the vehicle's wheels. Just one of the problems with this type of engine was finding a suitable fuel. Gunpowder was used in the seventeenth century, notably in the pump engines used to supply water to the gardens at the Palace of Versailles. A mixture of moss, coal-dust and resin powered the engine of a French boat in 1807, and the same year a Swiss engineer, François Isaac de Rivaz (1752–1828), ran an engine fuelled with hydrogen, using it to drive a four-wheeled vehicle. This is often described as the world's first internal combustion-engined car, although de Rivaz never developed his engine into a practical machine.

Coal gas was the fuel of choice for French engineer Jean Joseph Étienne Lenoir (1822–1900) in his engine in 1858, and by 1863 he had progressed to using petroleum. The previous year, another Frenchman, Alphonse Beau de Rochas (1815–1893), patented a four-stroke engine. There is no evidence to show that he actually built an engine based on his patent plans, but if he had this would have been the first engine to use what became the most widely adopted system of internal combustion. As the piston moves down inside the cylinder on its first "stroke", fuel and air are drawn into the cylinder. On the second (upward) stroke, the fuel and air are compressed, then ignited. The expanding gas from the explosion forces the piston downwards for its third stroke and the fourth (upward) stroke then clears the spent gases from the cylinder.

Gottlieb Daimler (1834–1900)

The son of a baker, Gottlieb Daimler was born in Schorndorf near Stuttgart. As a teenager, he studied to become a gunsmith but eventually decided that his future lay in the wider world of engineering. He worked as a draftsman in Geislingen before moving to Reutlingen in 1863, where he met his future business partner, Wilhelm Maybach. While at Deutz, the duo worked on Nikolaus Otto's four-stroke petrol engine, developing and improving it for use in vehicles once they parted company with Deutz. Daimler's ambition was to see his engines providing powered transport on land, at sea and in the air – the triumvirate concept that would lead to the adoption of the three-pointed star symbol by Daimler-Benz.

ABOVE Gottlieb Daimler's son, Paul, drives his father in the world's first four-wheeled car in 1886.

BELOW Maybach and Daimler first installed their engine in a wooden bicycle frame, creating the world's first motorbike in 1885.

Italian engineers Eugenio Barsanti (1821–1864) and Felice Matteucci (1808–1887) had presented their version of the internal combustion engine to the world in 1854 and by 1856 they were working on a two-cylinder version. Most of the engineers and inventors trying to perfect this new engine were doing so in order to find a way to replace steam power with a more efficient means of generating power for industry. While they were working on stationary engines, Gottlieb Daimler (see box feature page 8) and Wilhelm Maybach (1846–1929) were developing Nikolaus Otto's (1832–1891) version of the engine as a transport powerplant. The pair left Otto's Deutz company in 1882 to set up on their own in Stuttgart, where they were just a few kilometres away from the engine works of another engineer who shared their vision of powered transport – Karl Benz.

TOP A mid-19th century engraving of a steam carriage designed by Nicholas Cugnot and built in 1769. It is said to be the first self-propelled mechanical vehicle, here having the first automobile accident.

ABOVE The first steam-driven vehicle designed by the Frenchman Nicholas Joseph Cugnot.

Petrol Power

By 1885 Gottlieb Daimler and Wilhelm Maybach had developed a version of their engine with a carburettor supplying the fuel/air mix to the cylinder and had installed it in a wooden bicycle. Maybach rode the world's first motorbike for about 3 km (2 miles) along the bank of the Neckar River, reaching 11 kmph (7 mph). Unknown to them, Karl Benz had already gone one step further and installed his own engine in a tricycle machine. The single-cylinder engine could propel the Benz Patent Motorwagen up to 13 kmph (8 mph). It was a two-seater with large bicycle wheels running on solid rubber tyres. The engine drove the rear wheels, while the smaller front wheel steered the car.

BELOW, LEFT Karl Benz's 1886 tricycle was the first motor car to go on sale to the general public.

BELOW, RIGHT George Selden and Henry Ford in Selden's four-wheeled automobile.

Although tests on the track around Benz's factory went well, on its first public outing the car broke down. Benz managed to drive 0.8 km (half a mile) on his second venture out onto the public roads. In an effort to improve reliability, he then installed a more powerful engine and a second gear to improve speed. The new car was tested on the roads around Mannheim in the dead of night to avoid the embarrassment of people watching it grind to a halt. Eventually, the teething problems were ironed out and the car was put into production at Mannheim, reaching a level of 12 cars per week at one point. One of the first customers was Emile Roger (dates unknown), a bicycle manufacturer in Paris. He had been building Benz engines under licence and now became the sole agent for the Benz Motorwagen in France. The cars were also sold in England. In fact, well over a third of the early Benz cars were sold abroad, perhaps partly because it was still illegal in many parts of Germany to use machine-driven vehicles on the roads. Nor was it easy to refuel the cars – filling stations did not yet exist. Petrol (gasoline) could be bought in small quantities from pharmacists who stocked it as a cleaning agent.

Gottlieb Daimler (see box feature page 8), meanwhile, had progressed from his motorcycle experiment, buying a carriage into which he and Maybach installed a version of their engine, then taking to the roads in the world's first four-wheeled car powered by the internal combustion engine. The world's first, that is, only if you discount American pioneer George B Selden (1846–1922). Selden was a patent lawyer from New York who was fascinated by all things mechanical. Having seen a massive internal combustion engine on display in Philadelphia in 1876, he decided to design his own, smaller version, suitable for powering a carriage. He filed a patent for his four-wheeled car in 1879, seven years before the Benz patent was ratified, but he then tinkered with the plans, delaying the granting of his American patent until 1895. Selden did not put his design into production, although he did eventually establish his own car company. For a time he successfully claimed royalties from other American motor manufacturers: because he had patented the motor car, or "Road Engine", in America, other American car builders had to pay him a royalty for every vehicle they produced. Ultimately, Henry Ford led a consortium of manufacturers in a successful campaign to have Selden's royalty claims rejected in the law courts, although the legal battle raged until 1911.

German Patent No 37435

When Benz & Co applied for their patent for a gas-powered engine to be used in "light vehicles and small vessels to transport between one and four persons", Karl Benz and his associates could not have imagined that they were making history. By including the plans for Benz's skeletal tricycle "Motorwagen", however, they created a document that has been described as the "birth certificate" of the motorcar, making it an item of huge historical significance. The 1886 patent document, along with related Benz papers from the period, has since been recognised as historically important by UNESCO (United Nations Educational, Scientific and Cultural Organization) when it was inscribed in their register of World Documentary Heritage in May 2011, joining other documents of great significance like the Gutenberg Bible and the Magna Carta.

Karl Benz (1844–1929)

Hard work and a fascination for all things mechanical took Karl Friedrich Benz (later known as Carl) from a life of poverty in Karlsruhe, Germany, to the height of success as the founder of the world's first car company. Karl's mother, Josephine, was not married to his father, Johann, when their child was born, and she raised the child on her own when Johann, a locomotive driver, was killed in a railway accident two years later. Josephine's priority was to provide a good education for Karl and he eventually studied mechanical engineering at the University of Karlsruhe. He worked for a number of different engineering companies before establishing his own company, ultimately with financial assistance from his wife, Bertha, in Mannheim.

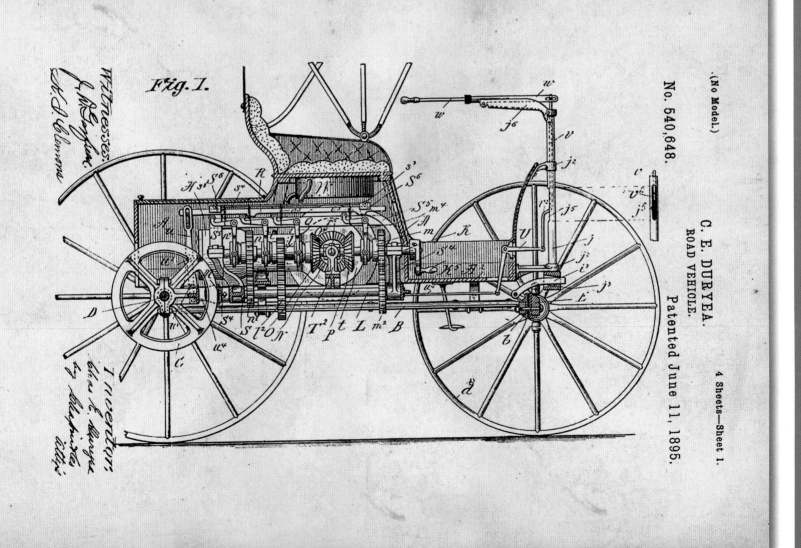

LEFT Charles Duryea became America's first volume manufacturer of motor cars.

BELOW This 1893 French Panhard et Lavassor car was powered by a Daimler engine.

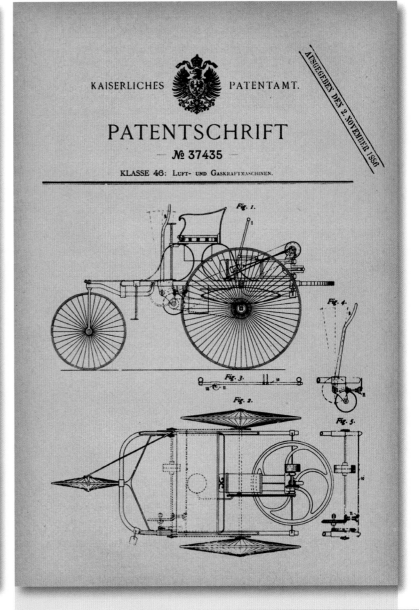

While Daimler and Maybach continued to refine and develop their engines, they did not limit themselves to powering motor cars. They built engines for use in motorboats and even powered an airship. In 1894, they also devised the first successful four-cylinder petrol engine, which set the benchmark for all others to follow. Peugeot and Panhard cars shared the honours in the world's first motor race in 1894, both powered by Daimler engines.

Across the Atlantic, Daimler engines were also making an impact in America. German-born piano manufacturer William Steinway (1835–1896) had acquired a licence to build Daimler engines in the United States, initially for stationary or marine use but with the motor-car market firmly in mind. The Daimler Motor Company, New York, was established in 1888. Taxes and shipping costs meant that importing European cars into America was very expensive, but domestic manufacturers were busy developing their home market with great enthusiasm. Charles (1861–1938) and Frank (1869–1967) Duryea had America's first four-wheeled, petrol-powered car running in 1893. By 1896, the Duryea Motor Wagon Company of Chicopee, Massachusetts had produced 15 identical motor cars.

In 1893 the Chief Engineer with the Edison Illuminating Company, Henry Ford (see box feature page 17), had produced his first petrol engine as a private venture. Three years later he had built his "Quadricycle" car which he sold for US$200, using the proceeds to begin building a more sophisticated vehicle. He founded the Detroit Automobile Company in 1899. Ford would become

The Duryea Patent

Germany may claim to have been the birthplace of the motorcar, but America was where it grew up, and the first American gas-powered automobile was built in 1893 by Charles and Frank Duryea. The brothers were bicycle manufacturers who became fascinated by the new horseless carriages, building their own first car in 1893 by buying a second-hand horse buggy, putting the horse out to grass and powering it with an internal combustion engine instead. They patented their four-wheel automobile in 1895 with Charles credited as the inventor. Five months later, Frank drove a Duryea automobile to victory in America's first organized motor race, ploughing through heavy snow between Chicago and Wukegan to finish the 86-kilometre (54-mile) course in 10 hours and 23 minutes.

famous for his production-line vehicle manufacturing techniques, but as the nineteenth century drew to a close it was Ransom Eli Olds (1864–1950), and his Oldsmobile Motor Works in Michigan, who was preparing to demonstrate how to mass produce cars.

Demand for petrol-powered cars was certainly there. Oil, previously harvested from holes in the ground into which it had seeped, mainly for use in lamps, began to be produced in vast quantities after the first oil well was drilled in Pennsylvania in 1859. Petrol power was poised to take over the world.

Into the Twentieth Century

The world sped into a new century with cars clattering, or chuffing, or gliding silently around its major cities. The petrol-engined car was to dominate the marketplace but steam vehicles would still be found huffing and puffing along the highways for at least another 20 years. There were many advantages to steam power. Once the problems of manufacturing a steam engine small enough for a car had been mastered, the steam car was actually a far more simple machine. It did not require the complex engineering and manufacturing processes of an internal combustion engine. The steam engine was far more robust and had far fewer moving parts, so there was less chance of it going wrong.

Steam vehicles were faster than other cars, too. The first motor race from Paris to Rouen in 1894 was actually won by a steam-powered tractor unit towing a carriage (see page 20). It was disqualified because the vehicle required a stoker, leaving the Daimler-powered Peugeots and Panhards to claim victory. The more sophisticated steam cars did not need the boiler to be stoked like a train or a ship's engine did, since the water in the boiler was heated using petrol- or kerosene-fired burners. A "Stanley Steamer" built in Massachusetts shattered the World Land Speed Record held by Henry Ford's 999 racer (147 kmph/91.37 mph), reaching 205.5 kmph (127.66 mph).

One of the drawbacks with steam power had been that the engines required regular top-ups of water, limiting the car's range. Condensers that captured the spent steam and returned it to the system as water helped to solve that problem. In any case, in the early days motor cars were only used around town as there were few good roads linking cities. The twentieth century was well underway before the road networks really began to spread outside urban areas. The real problem with steam, however, was that a steam-powered car simply took too long to get going. The boiler needed to be lit and the water heated to produce steam before you could go anywhere. That could take anything from 10 to 45 minutes.

Charles Stewart Rolls was the son of the Baron of Llangattock, whose family seat was a rambling Victorian country house in Monmouthshire, although Charles was born in Berkeley Square in London. Rolls graduated from Cambridge with a degree in Mechanical and Applied science. The Peugeot he had bought in 1896, when he was only 18, was the first car in Cambridge, and when he set up Britain's first car dealership in Fulham in 1903, he was supplying his customers with Peugeots from France and Minerva cars from Belgium. The photograph shows Rolls during the 1901 Paris-Berlin race driving a French Mors car and comes from one of Rolls' own photo albums. As well as his love for motoring, Rolls was also a pioneer aviator, making the first non-stop double crossing of the English Channel in June 1910. He died a month later in an accident during a flying display at Bournemouth.

LEFT A streamlined Stanley Steamer at Daytona in Florida in 1906 where it set the World Land Speed Record.

Henry Ford (1863–1947)

Having started life on a farm near Detroit, Henry Ford showed a keen interest in all things mechanical from an early age, building his first steam engine when he was only 15. He left home at the age of 17 to work as an apprentice machinist in Detroit but returned to the family farm three years later. He ran the portable steam engine and was eventually employed by the Westinghouse Company to service steam engines. He ran a saw-mill for a while before becoming an engineer with the Edison Illuminating Company. His experiments with internal combustion engines led him into the car business, although his first car company, the Detroit Automobile Company, went bankrupt in 1901. Two years later, he founded the Ford Motor Company.

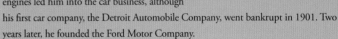

Starting a petrol-engined car was quicker, but could be frustratingly complicated. Even by the time Ford introduced its Model T in 1908, a vast improvement on the company's previous vehicles, one couldn't just walk out the front door, jump in the car and drive off. Starting the Model T meant using a variety of controls that would be a mystery to the modern driver. Behind the steering wheel – the thoroughly modern Model T had a steering wheel instead of the tiller arrangement that Ford's Quadricycle and most other very early cars employed – was the spark advance lever, which controlled the timing of the electrically generated sparks that ignited the fuel inside each of the engine's four cylinders. On the other side of the steering column from the spark advance was the hand throttle lever which controlled the speed of the engine. On the floor were three foot-pedals. If that sounds like a familiar arrangement, don't be fooled. The left pedal selected the two gears. Flat on the floor was slow and fully released was fast. Pushing the middle pedal threw the car into reverse and the right pedal was the foot brake. The hand brake lever also acted like a clutch to put the car in neutral or help you to select the fast gear.

To start the Model T, the spark advance and the throttle had to be set, making sure the hand brake was on (which put the car in neutral). The driver then walked round to the front of the car and set the choke by pulling on a cable beneath the radiator and primed the engine with a couple of gentle half-turns of the starting handle. A more forceful turn of the handle might then start the engine. If one neglected to set the other controls correctly, or the engine misfired, the starting handle could easily spin back with enough force to break a wrist. Nevertheless, this was still much quicker than waiting for a boiler to heat up.

LEFT Henry Ford's Model T was a thoroughly modern car, but there was an art to starting the engine that involved using controls that today's drivers wouldn't even recognize.

A popular choice for affluent city dwellers, especially in the United States, was the electric car. Electric cars did not smell of petrol or oil and did not sound as if they were attempting to shake themselves to pieces. They were clean and quiet, but their limited battery capacity meant that they also had a very limited range. This is a problem with which engineers and scientists are still struggling a century later. For city use, however, Studebaker built electric cars alongside their petrol-engined vehicles and, as with other electric car makers such as Riker or Fritchle, their vehicles were luxuriously appointed, costing up to US$3,000 at a time when the Model T cost just US$850. The Model T's price was set to drop dramatically as Ford's production techniques improved.

The ultimate in quiet-running, reliable, luxury motoring prior to the First World War came in 1906 with what *Autocar*, the world's oldest motoring magazine (established 1895), described as the "best car in the world" – the Rolls Royce Silver Ghost. The latest product from the factory of aristocratic motoring pioneer Charles Rolls (1877–1910) and engineer Henry Royce (1863–1933), the Silver Ghost boasted an advanced six-cylinder, 7-litre engine that ticked over at a barely audible whisper. The car cost US$5,000 – almost 10 times what a well-paid professional could expect to earn in a year – and that was just for the chassis. A coachbuilder then had to be commissioned to create the bodywork and interior trim.

OPPOSITE Charles Stewart Rolls in a French Mors car. Having set up his own company to import and sell French Peugeot and Belgian Minerva cars, Rolls became partners with motor manufacturer Henry Royce in 1904. A pioneer aviator, Rolls died aged 32 in 1910 when the tail of his Wright Flyer broke off during a display.

RIGHT Engineer Frederick Henry Royce used £20 savings to start a manufacturing company with a friend in 1884. Just over 20 years later he was making the most prestigious, high-quality motor cars in the world.

BELOW The Cadillac badge is based on the coat of arms of Antoine de la Mothe Cadillac, who founded the city of Detroit in 1701. One of his descendants, Henry Leland, established the company in 1902.

BOTTOM The very first Rolls Royce car to be called "Silver Ghost" was a 1907, silver-painted, 40–50 hp model, registration number AX 201, pictured here in 1961. Now owned by Bentley Motors, part of the Volkswagen group, the car is said to be one of the most valuable in the world with estimates ranging from £15 million to £50 million.

On the Starting Grid

The emerging motor industry produced a swarm of different car manufacturers, all competing for the attention of a growing throng of fledgling motorists. As these budding car drivers had to decide which particular vehicle merited them parting with a considerable amount of money, it quickly became clear that sporting events to showcase the virtues of individual vehicles would be ideal.

BELOW Émile Levassor at the controls of the Daimler-engined Panhard et Levassor that he drove to fourth place in the 1894 Paris–Rouen race.

In 1894, the French magazine *Le Petit Journal* organized the first motor race, although it was really more of a trial as cars were to be judged on speed and handling during the event rather than the first vehicle across the finishing line simply being declared the winner. Of the 69 vehicles that applied to join in the fun, only 25 made it through the 50-km (31-mile) selection run. These then set off to "race" 127 km (79 miles) from Paris to Rouen. First to arrive in Rouen was Count Jules-Albert de Dion (1856–1946) in a steam-powered car that was swiftly disqualified because it required a stoker. Three minutes and 30 seconds later, the first of a gaggle of Peugeots and Panhards arrived, the petrol-engined cars sharing the plaudits for having completed the course.

The following year, what is regarded as the first real race took place, although it was called the Paris–Bordeaux–Paris Trial. Émile Levassor (see box feature page 21), one of the esteemed finishers in the Paris–Rouen event, was the winner, covering the course in a time of 48 hours and 47 minutes. Levassor was supposed to swap with another driver when he reached Bordeaux, but he arrived hours before he was expected and no one could find his replacement. Pausing only to quaff a glass of champagne, he set off to drive the return leg to Paris, stopping at a restaurant 50 km (31 miles) outside the French capital for a meal in a restaurant.

Levassor's 48-hour marathon showed that cars and drivers were capable of covering long distances reliably, even on the poor roads of the nineteenth century,

Émile Levassor (1843–1897)

French engineer Émile Levassor began his career with a company that produced wood-working machines, which is where he met René Panhard (1841–1908). The two founded their own company in 1890, Panhard et Levassor, producing Daimler-engined cars. An enthusiastic racer, Levassor drove in the famous Paris–Rouen trial of 1894 and won the world's first real motor race the following year, finishing the Paris–Bordeaux contest six hours ahead of the second-placed driver. Levassor was badly hurt when he crashed while avoiding a dog in the Paris–Marseilles race of 1896 and died as a result of his injuries the following year.

and the publicity generated by motor racing helped to fill the manufacturers' order books. When Louis Renault (1877–1944) won the Paris–Toulouse–Paris race in 1900, the Renault company claimed that the victory generated 350 new orders at a time when the entire output of the company founded by Louis and his two brothers totalled just over half that number.

City-to-city races quickly grew in popularity, becoming more fast and furious as the performance of the cars improved. This brought an exciting spectacle to the public roads and with it, ever-increasing danger levels. Levassor was badly hurt in a crash in 1896; he never fully recovered and died the following year. Millionaire owner of *The New York Herald* Gordon Bennett (1841–1918) established an international trophy that was contested on roads in France, Austria, Germany and Ireland between 1900 and 1905, although latterly these races took place on organized road "circuits" rather than the open public highway. A race from Paris to Madrid in 1903 had highlighted the dangers of racing on public roads. Cars left Versailles at timed intervals, much as they

do in modern rally racing, and Louis Renault reached Bordeaux in under six hours, having reached 145 kmph (90 mph) at times. What he did not know was that his brother, Marcel (1872–1903), driving another Renault, had crashed and died on the road behind him. In fact, around half the cars had crashed by that stage, dozens of people had been injured and at least eight had been killed. One was a woman hit by a car as she ran across the road not far from Paris; a man and a child died when they were hit by a racer at Chatellerault and there were two fatalities among the spectators when a car crashed into a crowd of onlookers.

Other forms of racing flourished elsewhere. In the spring of each year, the French Riviera celebrated a speed week that included sprint races, a Concours d'Elegance presentation and build-quality competition in Monte Carlo; and, in 1897 at La Turbie near Nice, the world's first hill climb. Clearly, having the power to make it up a hill was important for any car and this was one of the biggest problems with the very first cars, where the driver and any passengers often had to dismount and

ABOVE The crashed Renault of Marcel Renault, who died during the 1903 Paris–Madrid road race. Dozens were injured and at least eight people died as cars crashed at speeds of up to 145 kmph (90 mph).

BELOW Louis Renault racing in the disastrous 1903 Paris–Madrid event. He led the field, not knowing that somewhere on the road behind him his brother had crashed and sustained fatal injuries.

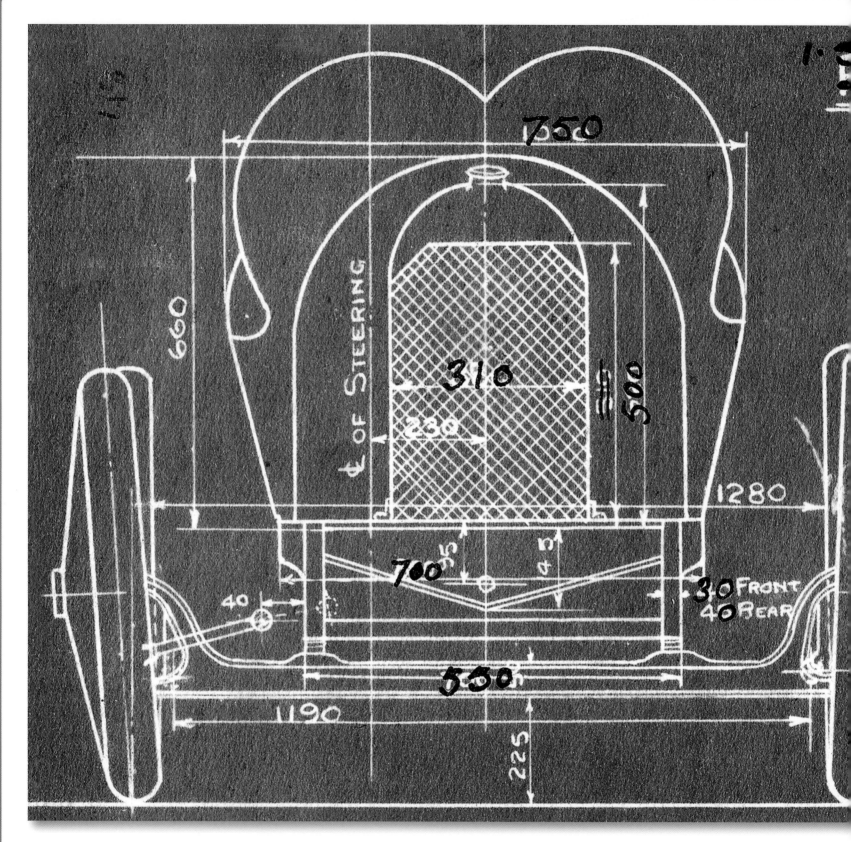

push if the gradient was too steep. It was in the Riviera events that diplomat and Daimler agent Emil Jellinek (1853–1918) swept the boards in 1901 with the special Daimler he had ordered from the factory and named after his daughter, Mercedes. The new 35-horsepower Mercedes created such a stir that one commentator from the French Automobile Club announced that "we have entered the Mercedes era" and Daimler officially registered the name.

Hill climbing became a hotly contested sport, and different types of event evolved. In Britain, the Shelsley Walsh hill climb has been run since 1905 and is something of a sprint at under a kilometre (907 metres/2,976 feet), while America's most famous hill climb is the Pikes Peak International. First run in 1916, the course starts on the Pikes Peak Highway in Colorado at an elevation of 2,862 metres (9,390 feet), rising through around 20 km (12.5 miles) of tarmac and gravel track, through 156 bends to a finish point at 4,298 metres (14,101 feet) – still a true test of any car's capabilities.

In 1906, Sicilian industrialist Vincenzo Florio (1883–1959) established one of Italy's most famous races, the Targa Florio, 446 km (277 miles) of hairpin bends in the mountains above Palermo. There were only a few motor manufacturers active in Italy at that time, although Fiat came into being that year, but the first race was won by an

CHASSIS

FRONT VIEW

WHEELBASE			2200
TRACK			1100
WHEELS			710 / 100.89
THICKNESS OF	MAIN FRAME		4 m.m
	UNDER FRAME		4 1/4 m.m
WIDTH OF FRONT SPRING			40
REAR "			50
DEPTH OF FRONT SPRING			28
" REAR "			33
LENGTH OF SHACKLE			60
CAPAC-TY OF PETROL TANK			80 1/2 LITRES
" " OIL TANK			20 LITRES
FULL LOCK			65°
1 COMPLETE REV. OF STEERING WHEEL MOVES LEVER			60°

(handwritten annotations) Cross members 6 leaves Depth 28 6 m/m thick eye 14 m/m — 7 leaves 6 m/m thick eye 16 1/2

eye are forged solid with main leaf.

Georges Roesch Blueprint

Georges Henry Roesch was a Swiss engineer born in Geneva in 1891. He worked in the motor industry in France before becoming Chief Engineer at Clement-Talbot in London in 1916. He remained with the company through the changes that saw its acquisition by French manufacturer Darracq in 1919 and a merger with British carmaker Sunbeam to become Sunbeam-Talbot-Darracq (STD) in 1920. Roesch was involved in a number of engineering innovations, including engine designs for new high-performance road cars, but his influence was most keenly felt in the STD Grand Prix cars where Peugeot designs from before the First World War were adapted to create successful racing machines, as shown in the annotated blueprint from Roesche's notebook. Roesch died in 1969.

Italian car – the monstrous 14.8-litre, five-cylinder Itala driven by Alessandro Cagno.

While racing on public roads continued at various events, the world's first purpose-built motor racing circuit was being planned at Brooklands, near Weybridge in England. The concrete track, which was 100 metres (328 feet) wide, had two huge banked sections where the outside edge of the track was 10 metres (33 feet) above the inside in an effort to prevent cars travelling at high speed from hurtling off the circuit. The track opened in 1907 and, several days prior to its inaugural race, Brooklands was used to set a world 24-hour endurance record when Selwyn Francis Edge (1868–1940) drove continuously for 2,544 km (1,581 miles) in his Napier at an average speed of 106 kmph (66 mph). His record stood for the next 17 years.

Track racing in America was already underway by 1907 at the Milwaukee Mile circuit. The oval track was originally intended for horse racing but its first motorsports event was held in 1903 and by 1910 the Milwaukee Mile was creating legends such as Barney Oldfield (1878–1946), who lapped the track in 1910 at an average speed of over 113 kmph (70 mph) in his "Blitzen Benz". By then, motor racing had established itself as an international sport that would act as a catalyst for the development of the motor car over the next hundred years.

24

OPPOSITE Daimler agent Emil Jellinek was Austrian Consul-General in Nice and a highly successful businessman when he asked Daimler to produce a car that was lower, longer and more powerful to compete in hill-climb trials. The result was the race-winning 35-hp model which he named "Mercedes" after his daughter.

RIGHT Reigning champion Vincenzo Lancia at the wheel of his Fiat during the 1905 Coppa Florio race at Brescia. Having won outright the previous year, Lancia finished third in this race.

BELOW American race ace Barney Oldfield at the wheel of the Lightning Benz (later re-branded as "Blitzen Benz") at Daytona in 1910. The 21.5-litre, 200-hp car was designed to exceed 200kmph (125 mph), which Oldfield did on his first outing with the car, reaching 212 kmph (131.7 mph), faster than any train or aircraft of the time.

Cars for Every Family

Gone were the days when cars were limited by law to no more than walking pace in town and gone, too, were the days when, in Britain, a man carrying a red flag had to walk ahead to warn other road users that a motor vehicle was approaching! Cars continued to share the roads with horse-drawn vehicles in major cities, but the horses were now increasingly used for hauling goods, wagons or public buses, those who once travelled by private carriage now preferring mechanical horsepower. Innovations abounded, with wire wheels taking the place of wooden "cart" wheels (although Benz [see page 8] had used wire bicycle-type wheels on his tricycle), shod with pneumatic tyres from Michelin, Dunlop or Goodyear.

In 1914, Cadillac introduced the type 51 with a new V-8 engine. The type 51 was superseded by the type 53 in 1916, a car that had electric starting (no more broken wrists with the starting handle); electric lights; the handbrake and gear lever in the middle, between the driver's and passenger's seats; and three pedals on the floor – clutch on the left, brake in the middle, accelerator on the right. This basic layout, instantly recognizable to today's drivers, was not immediately adopted as standard across the industry, although the luxury and engineering of the Cadillacs was much admired. Cadillac had its roots in the Henry Ford Motor Company (see page 17), which Henry Ford had left after a dispute with his partners in 1902. Engineer and entrepreneur

BELOW The Cadillac Type 53 of 1916 was the first car in the world to adopt the layout for the driver's controls that is still in general use today.

OPPOSITE Unveiled in Paris in 1900, this electric car driven by motors in the wheel hubs was designed by 25-year-old Ferdinand Porsche. He would go on to produce a car with a motor in each wheel for 4WD and a petrol generator to recharge the batteries – the world's first hybrid car in 1901.

Henry Leland (1843–1932) was brought in to run the old Henry Ford Company, renaming it Cadillac after the founder of Detroit. Cadillac became the luxury division of General Motors when Leland sold it to the conglomerate in 1909.

Ford, meanwhile, resisted introducing new changes to his own product for as long as possible. His philosophy was to mass produce the parts for his Model T and streamline the production process to drive the retail price of the Model T down to a level that everyone earning a reasonable wage could afford. Changes to the Model T were introduced gradually, but the casual observer would be hard pressed to spot the differences between the early cars produced in 1908 and the final versions that rolled off the production line almost 20 years later. The Model T had gone from 11 cars produced in the first month to one produced every three minutes, culminating in over 15 million being built. As well as in Detroit, the car was assembled in Britain, Germany, France, Argentina, Spain, Denmark, Norway, Belgium, Brazil, Mexico and Japan. Mass production brought the price down from US$850 to US$240 and at one time, half the cars in the world were Model Ts.

Ransom Olds (1864–1950), founder of the Oldsmobile and REO marques, can be said to have first introduced mass production to the motor industry with his "Curved Dash" Oldsmobile of 1904, but Ford took the concept to a new level, with moving production lines and workers specializing in specific areas. The majority of cars in the early twentieth century were painstakingly hand built by craftsmen but the cost benefits of mass production were plain to see. The "Curved Dash" Oldsmobile cost just US$650.

In Europe, the first motor manufacturer to use mass-production techniques was Citroën in 1919. Within 10 years the company was to become the world's fourth-largest car maker, rubbing shoulders with the likes of General Motors. Founded in 1908 by salesman and carriage builder William Crapo Durant (1861–1947), the GM corporation grew from consisting of just Buick to include Oldsmobile, Cadillac, Cartercar, Elmore, Ewing and Oakland, which later became Pontiac. Durant was ousted from GM management in 1910 and started Chevrolet along with the Swiss/American racing driver Louis Chevrolet (1878–1941). The success of Chevrolet allowed Durant to buy his way back into GM, taking his Chevrolet company with him.

OPPOSITE Having fitted pneumatic tyres to a car that they built themselves for the 1895 Paris–Bordeaux–Paris race, the Michelin brothers were at the forefront of tyre development and Bibendum, the character they developed to promote their tyres, boasted they could "defy every attack".

BELOW Interior of the Ford works, Trafford Park, Manchester, c1911-c1927. Rows of Model Ts are lined up. The hugely successful Model T was Britain's best-selling car from 1913 to 1923. The factory began assembling cars from imported parts in 1911, but by 1924 the vehicles were being constructed from 94% British parts.

While mergers, takeovers and partnerships were forged among the 200 or so motor manufacturers in America, a few chose to take a different route, not only with their organization but also with their products. Electric cars continued to sell and, as late as 1916, companies such as Woods in Chicago and Baker in Cleveland were offering petrol-electric hybrids, a concept that had first emerged in 1901 with Ferdinand Porsche's (1875–1951) "Mixte Hybrid", in which a petrol engine drove a generator that supplied power to four electric motors in the wheel hubs. Hybrids, however, fell by the wayside as petrol became cheaper and engineers designed multi-cylinder petrol engines that became more powerful, smoother and more reliable.

The Italian engineer Ettore Bugatti (1881–1947) combined a pursuit of excellence with an eye for beauty in his designs. Coming from a family of artists and craftsmen, he had a creative flair that did not fully flourish when he made cars for companies like de Dietrich or Deutz. In 1910 the 28-year-old set up his own operation at Molsheim in Alsace (then in Germany) and his Type 13 gave birth to a legend as the first thoroughbred Bugatti.

OPPOSITE Citroën began using mass-manufacturing techniques in 1919 and by the time this photo of A-type cars on the production line was taken in 1922, the company was well on the way to becoming the world's fourth-largest car maker.

BELOW The Bugatti works' driver Ernest Friderich at the wheel of one of a Type 13 racing car winning at Le Mans in August 1920. Ettore Bugatti focused on engineering excellence and beautiful design but also knew that weight was his enemy. The lighter the car, the faster it would go.

André-Gustav Citroën (1878–1935)

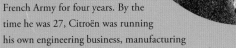

The man who mass produced armaments for the French military during the First World War and went on to establish what swiftly became France's largest car manufacturer was actually the son of a Dutch father and Polish mother. The word *citroen* means "lemon" in Dutch and Citroën's grandfather sold lemons, although his father was a diamond merchant. André was born after the family moved to Paris and he studied engineering at the military-run Ecole Polytechnique before joining the French Army for four years. By the time he was 27, Citroën was running his own engineering business, manufacturing gears. The double-chevron Citroën logo derives from the helical teeth on the gears the company produced. Citroën died of stomach cancer at the age of 57.

The Car Goes to War

Gräf & Stift is an Austrian company perhaps better known for its trucks and buses than its cars but, up to around 1938, it had a reputation for building luxurious automobiles much favoured by the Austrian aristocracy. In December 1910, Lieutenant Colonel Count Franz von Harrach (1870–1934) purchased a Gräf & Stift Double Phaeton limousine. Four years later the car hit the headlines in Sarajevo when Archduke Franz Ferdinand (1863–1914) and his wife, Sophie (1868–1914), were shot dead in its rear seat. The Count had been assigned as Franz Ferdinand's bodyguard but could not stop the determined young Bosnian assassin. The murder of the Archduke precipitated a chain of events that led to the outbreak of the First World War.

The Gräf & Stift can thus be regarded as the first car involved in what was the most highly mechanized war to be waged up to that point in history. Some military planners expected that the battlefields of the war that began in 1914 would be constantly shifting conflicts, with troops and equipment more mobile than ever before. That vision was not borne out in reality, although motorized transport played an enormous part in the proceedings. The British Army was the fighting force most comprehensively equipped with motor vehicles at the outset of the war. The Army Service Corps Mechanical Transport Companies ran fleets of trucks of various sizes along with a few motorcycles and saloon cars, all militarized versions of civilian designs or adapted from civilian vehicles. These were used for transporting supplies, but trucks and other commercial vehicles found many other uses – as ambulances, for example or, later in the war, as mobile platforms for anti-aircraft guns.

OPPOSITE Archduke Franz Ferdinand and his wife, Sophie, leave the Sarajevo Senate House in the rear seats of the Gräf & Stift limousine in which they were assassinated a few minutes later.

ABOVE Several Minerva cars such as the one above were converted into armoured vehicles and used as scout cars, creating havoc amongst the horses of the German cavalry formations.

The concept of mobile warfare, however, encompassed the idea of using vehicles not only for transport but also as offensive weapons. Cars armed with heavy machine guns could take the fight to the enemy, providing commanders with a swift and manoeuvrable strike force. British engineer Frederick Simms (1863–1944) produced his "Motor War Car" as early as 1902. It had all-round armour, a crew of four, two Maxim machine guns and a Daimler engine that could power it to 14.5 kmph (9 mph), but it was not adopted by the military. The first soldiers actually to use armoured cars in combat were Italian when Italy went to war with Turkey in 1911. A variety of armed and armoured Fiat trucks were shipped to Libya during this conflict but the first true armoured car to see action was an Isotta Frashini. Enveloped in 4-mm (0.16-inch) armour plate, the car had one Maxim gun mounted in its hull and another in a rotating turret. Renowned for its sports cars, Isotta Frashini provided enough power from its engine to propel the three-ton beast at up to 59.5 kmph (37 mph).

During the First World War, it was the Belgians who first made use of the armoured car. Lieutenant Charles Henkart (dates unknown) had his two Minerva cars fitted with armour and used them as scout cars. Minerva, known for producing luxury cars, designed an armour pattern to utilize the chassis from its 38-horsepower tourer. The cars were armed with Hotchkiss machine guns or 37-mm (1.46-inch) cannon. Peugeot, Renault, Lancia and the British luxury car maker Lanchester (see box feature page 35) all produced armoured cars during the course of the war, although none was as huge as the Germans' monstrous Erhardt E-V/4. With their cavalry having suffered from the hit-and-run tactics of the Belgian Minervas during the early phase of the war, the Germans decided to produce their own armoured car. The result was a huge vehicle weighing up to nine tons with a crew of eight and armed with three machine guns. It had double wheels at the back to try to help stop it sinking into the ground and, crucially, four-wheel drive.

Four-wheel drive was proving essential for military vehicles serving on the Western Front as the mobile battlefield settled down into the long slog of trench warfare. Deeply rutted muddy tracks were a nightmare for all mechanized transport. Four-wheel drive helped and the Four Wheel Drive Auto Company of Wisconsin provided US and British forces with 15,000 of its 4x4 trucks while the Jeffery company, also of Wisconsin, supplied 11,500 of its Quad trucks that had four-wheel drive, four-wheel brakes and four-wheel steering. Nevertheless, in rough terrain or deep mud, horses still proved more reliable. Armoured cars, of course, were of little use on muddy battlefields strewn with trenches. Where they did come into their own was in the open plains on the Eastern Front, which is where the giant Erhardts saw most of their wartime service, or in the vast expanses of desert in the Middle East.

In 1914, all available chassis for the Rolls Royce Silver Ghost had been requisitioned for the production of a new armoured car, but by the time these entered service there was little use for them on the Western Front. Instead, many ended up in the Middle East where Lawrence of Arabia (1888–1935) acquired one for use against the Turks. He was later quoted as saying that "a Rolls in the desert is above rubies" and told one journalist who asked him about his heart's desire: "I should like my own Rolls-Royce car with enough tyres and petrol to last me all my life."

OPPOSITE Lawrence of Arabia was a devotee of the Rolls Royce as an armoured car for desert operations, although he is pictured here driving a Talbot.

BELOW A Rolls Royce armoured car parked in the street in Arras in 1917.

Frederick Lanchester (1868–1946)

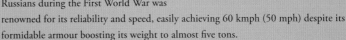

For a man who was later revered as a scientist, engineer and inventor, Frederick Lanchester showed little promise as a scholar while at school in Brighton. He had no formal educational qualifications when he started his first job as a draughtsman with the Patent Office. Nevertheless, Lanchester went on to design engines with revolutionary features such as twin crankshafts that allowed smoother running and he experimented with fuel injection and turbo-chargers. By the time he was producing Lanchester cars, his vehicles were rivalled only by Rolls Royce. The Lanchester armoured car that saw service with the British, Belgians and Russians during the First World War was renowned for its reliability and speed, easily achieving 60 kmph (50 mph) despite its formidable armour boosting its weight to almost five tons.

The Racing Twenties

America's automotive giants Ford and GM knew that a serious contender was stepping into the ring with them when Walter Chrysler (1875–1940) began building cars bearing his own name in 1924. Chrysler had previously been employed by GM and attempted to resign when William C Durant (1861–1947) took over in 1916. Durant, however, decided that he needed Chrysler, offering him the phenomenal salary of US$10,000 per month plus an annual bonus of US$500,000 if he would stay and run Buick. Chrysler stayed for three more years.

By the time Walter Chrysler left GM, selling his shares in the company, he was one of America's richest men. He spent two years in charge of the Willys-Overland Motor Company, failing in his attempt to buy the business, before purchasing Maxwell Motors and setting up his own Chrysler, Plymouth and DeSoto marques to establish the Chrysler Corporation in 1925. In 1928, Chrysler also bought Dodge, confirming his status as one of the motor industry's major players. The first Chrysler, launched at the New York Automobile Show in January 1924 and marketed by Maxwell Motors, had a new six-cylinder engine fitted with a smooth-running, seven-bearing crankshaft, an air filter for the carburettor, an oil filter and four-wheel hydraulic brakes. These were features that had never before been seen on a medium-priced car and sales for the first year snowballed to 32,000. Within two years, Chrysler was building 1,250 cars per day, making them the sixth-largest manufacturer in the United States, with sales rising and the model range expanding. Chryslers, like most other marques, now looked far more robust than previous cars. The bodywork enclosed the passengers more securely so that you sat inside the car rather than riding on it. The mudguards covering the front wheels swept down to running boards that ran back to the rear wheel-arch bulges,

ABOVE The MG Midget, seen here taking part in a time trial race, helped to establish Britain's reputation for producing competitive sports cars.

OPPOSITE The Austin Seven, launched in 1922, was an affordable car that quickly became a much-loved, family-car success. Although smaller than Ford's Model T, it could, as shown here, carry up to five people!

Giovanni Agnelli (1866–1945)

In 1899, the mayor of Villar Perosa, a small town in Piedmont in Italy, joined with a group of like-minded investors to set up a new car company in Turin. Giovanni Agnelli had studied in Turin and enjoyed a brief military career before deciding to put his engineering skills to use in 1899 with the Fabbrica Italiana di Automobili Torino, better known nowadays as Fiat. Agnelli invested US$400 in the new company – far less than the cost of one new car at the time – and became the managing director within a year. By 1920, Agnelli was Chairman of Fiat and weathered all sorts of industrial unrest, including an attempted Communist Workers' takeover, to see his company become one of Europe's most important manufacturers. Agnelli continued to take an active role in Fiat, including the rebuilding of its war-damaged facilities, right up to his death in December 1945.

giving passengers a "footstep" to help make getting in and out of the vehicle easier. It was on these running boards that Chicago gangsters (at least in the movies) perched while spraying their rivals with bullets from their "Tommy" guns. The gangsters' violent clashes led to some unique modifications of standard cars. Al Capone (1899–1947) owned several Cadillacs (bought in the name "Mr Brown"), at least one of which, a 1928 Town Sedan, was modified with heavy armour plate behind the body panels, newly-developed 2.5-cm- (1-inch-) thick bullet-proof glass, flashing red lights behind the radiator grille, a police-band radio receiver and a police siren. The car was confiscated by the US Treasury Department when Capone was convicted of tax evasion in 1931. Ten years later the car was still in the government's possession and, following the Japanese attack on Pearl Harbor, the Secret Service pressed the armoured Cadillac into service to protect President Roosevelt (1882–1945).

Although not quite the bullet-proof quality of Capone's Cadillac, by the 1920s laminated glass was being used in car windscreens. The horrendous injuries caused to drivers and their passengers in car crashes when they were hurled through windscreens made of ordinary window glass led to laminated safety glass being adopted, with Ford installing safety glass on all its new cars, including the all-new Model T replacement, the Model A, in 1927. Within two weeks of Ford unveiling

their new product, they had 400,000 orders on their books. On a far smaller scale, the first of a make of motor car designed to withstand the rigours of a Swedish winter was also launched in 1927 – the Volvo ÖV4 "Jakob". Less than a thousand Jakobs were built in the first year.

Car production in America, on the other hand, was booming. In 1920 there were eight million cars on America's roads, a number which grew to 28 million by the end of the decade. People were buying new cars with credit agreements arranged through the manufacturers. GM introduced the first of these with its General Motors Acceptance Corporation, which allowed purchasers to spread the burden of buying their cars using affordable monthly payments. Banks had previously been reluctant to lend money for people to buy cars. GM President Alfred Sloan (1875–1966) adopted a pricing structure that took buyers from the cheaper end of the range with Chevrolet, through Pontiac, Oldsmobile and Buick to GM's expensive luxury brand, Cadillac. The intention was to keep buyers within the GM "family" as their careers progressed and their spending power increased. Sloan also introduced the concept of "planned obsolescence" making styling changes across the range every year so that a 1929 Buick would look different to a 1928 Buick, encouraging customers to replace their vehicles regularly to save themselves the humiliation of being seen driving last year's model. It was a policy that other manufacturers were quick to follow.

While American manufacturers raced ahead with innovative engineering and ever-increasing production levels, in 1923 several levels of production were achieved in Italy within one building. The new Fiat car plant at Ligotto in Turin (see box feature page 37) was built on five floors, and the whole plant was a moving production line. Components and materials went into the factory on the ground floor and finished cars were driven out onto the oval rooftop test track. It was the largest car plant in the world, producing a range of models such as the 509 which,

having sold 90,000 units, helped to boost Fiat's share of the Italian car market to a massive 87 per cent.

The general layout of a car's controls had, by the middle of the 1920s, adopted the style that we know today. The Austin Seven of 1922 helped to popularize the layout used by Cadillac on their Type 53 in 1916, taking the tradition of clutch, brake and accelerator on the floor and handbrake and gearstick between the seats to a far wider market. The Austin was smaller than Ford's Model T and affordable at £165. It became a huge success and was built under licence in Germany as the first BMW. As the "Dixie" in 1927, it was licensed for manufacture in America and France and also became the basis for Nissan's first cars in Japan.

In 1929, the founding father of the automobile business, Karl Benz (see box feature, page 11), died aged 84. Despite the fact that they had lived and worked in the same area of Germany, Benz never met Gottlieb Daimler (see box feature, page 8), who had died in 1900, although difficult economic circumstances in Germany led to their names being united when their companies merged in 1926 as Daimler-Benz, with their cars manufactured under the now legendary brand name of Mercedes-Benz. Karl Benz remained active on the board of Daimler-Benz up to his death.

PREVIOUS PAGES New Fiats, having entered the ground floor of the innovative factory in Turin as raw materials and components, are tested on the roof-top track in 1929.

ABOVE Walter P Chrysler shakes hands with his company's Vice President, Bernard Edwin Hutchinson, in 1934 as Hutchinson drives the millionth Plymouth (the first one was produced in 1928) off the production line.

OPPOSITE The forerunner of Renault's famous diamond logo was first seen on the front of their 9.1-litre 40 CV model in 1925.

RENAULT
La 40 cv Sport

Power and Glory

By the 1920s, motor racing had become far better organized than the road-racing chaos that had preceded it. The first race regularly using the name "Grand Prix" was staged by the Automobile Club de France at Le Mans in 1906. The race took place on a 103-km (64-mile) circuit on public roads that were closed for the duration of the event. By 1923, the Le Mans race had developed into a 24-hour Grand Prix of Endurance that was one of the most prestigious of all international motor racing events.

The 1923 event was won by French drivers André Lagache (1885–1938) and René Léonard (dates unknown) in a French Chenard et Walcker car, but the maker that was to dominate the event throughout the 1920s was Bentley. The huge green Bentleys ranged in engine size from 3.0 litres to 6.5 litres, winning in 1924 and every year from 1926 to 1930 against stiff competition from Mercedes-Benz and Alfa Romeo. Le Mans was undoubtedly a glamorous event, with wealthy young men such as Woolf Barnato (1895–1948), who won three consecutive Le Mans races driving for the Bentley team, becoming household names. The Bentley drivers were known as "The Bentley Boys" to the British public, although to those who regarded motor racing as an indulgence enjoyed by rich hedonists, the term was more pejorative than respectful.

Although it was a Grand Prix, Le Mans was not always the French Grand Prix. Grand Prix was a name used for the most important international events in the motor racing calendar and different circuits were used to host the races when they were staged as international events. The first Grand Prix World Championship

OPPOSITE American racing driver Jimmy Murphy powers his 3-litre Duesenberg to victory at the Le Mans French Grand Prix in 1921.

ABOVE The European Grand Prix, an honorary designation awarded to one of the European races each year, was held for the first time at Monza in Italy in 1923. The modern European Grand Prix has taken place each year since 2008 at Valencia in Spain.

was organized in 1925 as a manufacturers' competition consisting of five Grands Prix which included the Indianapolis 500, the Belgian Grand Prix at Spa-Francorchamps, the Italian Grand Prix at Monza and the French race at Montlhéry. The Championship was won by Alfa Romeo with their P2 racing car, although their star driver, Antonio Ascari (1888–1925), was killed while leading the French Grand Prix.

The race track at Indianapolis had opened in 1909 with races attracting crowds of up to 40,000 spectators but when attendance numbers started to fall away the following year, the track's owners opted to promote one very special event. They

considered an endurance race like Le Mans, but eventually opted for a 805-km (500-mile) race and the first Indianapolis 500 was staged in May 1911. The race offered a top prize of US$25,000 and 80,000 spectators turned out to watch Ray Harroun (1879–1968) romp home in his Marmon Wasp racer.

Indianapolis (affectionately known as Indy) was a purpose-built race track, whereas Le Mans and Spa-Francorchamps used closed sections of public roads to stage their Grands Prix. The Italian Grand Prix at Monza was held on a specially designed circuit from 1922, much to the chagrin of the people of Brescia, who had hosted the first Italian Grand Prix in 1921 and previously the Coppa Florio.

Determined to preserve their racing heritage, some wealthy enthusiasts financed a road race from Brescia to Rome and back, a distance of 1,500 km (roughly 1,000 Roman miles) and the famous Mille Miglia was born. The race was a return to the open-road, city-to-city roots of motor racing and the inaugural event took place in March 1927 in torrential rain. All of the participants were Italian and the race became a battle between the mighty Alfa P2s and a team of three "local" OM Tipo 665s, built in Brescia. The OMs were ultimately triumphant, taking first, second and third places with an average speed over the mountainous course of more than 77 kmph (48 mph).

While the Italians were coaxing more power from ever more sophisticated engines with the 2-litre, eight-cylinder, supercharged Alfa P2, the hugely successful Fiat Tipo 805 2-litre and the 2-litre OMs – all developed to compete in 2-litre Grand Prix races – the Americans had traditionally looked to bigger engines for more power. The 1921 French Grand Prix at Le Mans (not the 24-hour race) had been won by racing driver Jimmy Murphy (1894–1924) in a 3-litre Duesenberg. Duesenberg had a reputation for excellence in producing road cars with engines of 6 litres or more that were fast and luxurious, giving rise to the appreciative phrase "It's a Duesy". The engineering skills required to produce racing cars with smaller engines were not unknown in the United States, however. When a new 2-litre formula was introduced for the Indianapolis 500 in 1923, an engineer who had made a name for himself in racing, Harry Miller (1875–1943), designed a world-class engine and a car that won the race. Jimmy Murphy's Duesenberg at Le Mans had run with a larger Miller engine and also won at Indy the previous year. Miller's cars and engines were to dominate races across America, especially the Indianapolis 500. When the engine size for the Indy 500 was further restricted to 1,500 cc,

Enzo Ferrari (1898–1988)

As a youth, Enzo Ferrari watched motor races with his father, and his heroes were racing drivers like Vincenzo Lancia (1881–1937), driving state-of-the-art Fiat racers. The young Enzo acquired a sound understanding of mechanics as his father's metalwork business evolved into a car repair shop. Following a medical discharge from the Italian Army, Enzo quickly found work in the car business, even though he had no formal training as an engineer, and by 1920 he was testing and racing cars for Alfa Romeo. He notched up a few notable successes, but his real talent lay in managing the racing team and the development of its cars. In 1929, he set up Scuderia Ferrari to manage Alfa's racing endeavours; the Ferrari name would forever more be associated with racing and sports cars.

OPPOSITE Pete DePaolo in the Miller "Flying Cloud Special" that he drove at Indianapolis in 1928. DePaolo won the first US Grand Prix at Indianapolis in 1925, driving a Duesenberg.

Monte Carlo Rally Poster, 1930

Monte Carlo is bathed in sunshine, looking almost tropical, a welcoming sight for the driver of the car racing through the snowy mountains to reach the seaside paradise. Note the spade strapped on top of the other equipment on the running board of the car. The Monte Carlo Rally was such a prestigious race because it provided such a severe test for the participating cars and their drivers. The weather in January could easily be pleasantly warm by the coast but bitterly cold in the mountains and any manufacturer who could boast that their car had won the Monte could claim to offer a truly reliable vehicle. The winner in 1930 was Hector Petit driving a French Licorne, with Al Berlesco second in a DeSoto and A. Blin D'Orimont third in a Studebaker. The poster was painted by renowned French artist and illustrator Robert Falcucci (1900–1989) who was an official French military artist as well as creating advertising art for champagne, holiday posters and Formula One racing.

Miller came up with another winner, taking first place at Indianapolis from 1926 to 1929. During those years, three-quarters of the cars starting the Indy 500 would be Millers or Miller-engined racers. Winning meant racing a Miller, but it didn't come cheap. A standard Miller car cost US$10,000 and his innovative front-wheel-drive racer of 1924 was US$15,000.

The first German Grand Prix was held at the AVUS circuit south of Berlin in 1926 where Remagen-born Rudolf Caracciola (1901–1959) took the title driving a Mercedes-Benz in heavy rain, earning him the title Regenmeister, or Rain Master. Caracciola and Mercedes also won the inaugural race at the Nürburgring in 1927, although he lost the German Grand Prix title there a month later due to mechanical failure. Caracciola regained his German Grand Prix title the following year. The Germans had never adopted the international Grand Prix engine-size limits, so in 1928 Caracciola had the joy of winning on home territory in the magnificent, brand-new 7.1-litre Mercedes-Benz SS, designed by Ferdinand Porsche.

OPPOSITE Giuseppe Campari and Giulio Ramponi on their way to victory in the 1928 Mille Miglia driving an Alfa Romeo 6C 1500 Sport Spider Zagato.

RIGHT Woolf Barnato and Sir Henry "Tim" Brikin leave Jack Dunfee and Glen Kidston looking up their exhaust pipe as the two Bentley Speed 6 cars finish first and second at Le Mans in 1929.

BELOW Rudolf Caracciola won the German Grand Prix at the Nürburgring in 1931 with the Mercedes-Benz SSKL. The "L" stood for *leicht* meaning lightweight, the car having even had holes drilled in its chassis to save weight.

The New Style Era

The dawn of the 1930s was the beginning of a whole new age of automobile design. Mass-production techniques meant that car bodies were now being supplied straight from the factory as an integral part of the car's design – and car design was becoming ever more sophisticated. While most of the many millions of cars on the roads in Britain, throughout Europe and in the United States in the early 1930s still sported carriage-style mudguards shielding the wheels, the new style era was about to shatter the car's links with its horse-drawn predecessor.

In 1935 Bugatti (see page 31) unveiled the Aerolithe Electron Coupé prototype at the Paris Auto Salon. The show car spawned what many describe as the most beautiful of all pre-war automobiles, the Bugatti Type 57 SC Atlantic. The styling owes more to the aircraft industry than it does to traditional coachbuilding techniques, with the guards over the tyres flowing into the bodywork, enclosing the wheels in much the same way that the fixed undercarriage of aircraft at that time were streamlined. The "fin" that ran down the roof to the sloping tail and the external riveting on the panels, used because the special lightweight alloy could not be welded, all added to the aircraft feel. The speed was almost aircraft-like as well, the 200-brake horsepower, eight-cylinder engine propelling the low-slung coupé to over 193 kmph (120 mph). Bugatti was not the only manufacturer daring to follow aviation's styling cues. Mercedes sports cars were displaying sleek, flowing lines, although none as sleek as the W125 Rekordwagen used to set the world speed record on a public road in 1938 at 431 kmph (268 mph). The Rekordwagen was not, of course, a car designed for everyday road use, unlike BMW's 328 of 1936. This elegant sports car had headlamp housings that were integral to the front wings rather than standing proud like carriage lamps.

ABOVE This Mercedes W125 Rekordwagen still holds the record for the fastest speed ever recorded on a public road. On 28 January 1938, Rudolph Caracciola reached a top speed of 431 kmph (268 mph) over a flying kilometre on the autobahn between Frankfurt and Darmstadt, Germany.

Some of the most sensational styling and technical innovations, however, were happening in America. The Chrysler Airflow of 1934 was famously the first American production car to use streamlining, but it was not an elegant design and the American public simply didn't like it. Perhaps it was better appreciated in Japan, where Toyota's first car, the AA in 1936, was remarkably similar to the Airflow. Other US manufacturers had more success with state-of-the-art styling. While Bugatti were displaying their Aerolithe in Paris, Auburn redesigned their 1933 Speedster model as the fabulous 1935 851 Boattail Speedster. The supercharged V-8 cars all carried a plaque confirming that they had been test driven at speeds in excess of 160 kmph (100 mph).

The most remarkable car to emerge from the Auburn stable around this time, however, was the Cord 810. It caused a sensation when it was launched at the 1935 New York Auto Show, not only for its streamlined styling but also for its technical innovations. It had variable-speed windscreen wipers at a time when many cars had no wipers or, if they did, wipers that were operated by hand. It had retractable headlights, front-wheel drive and a dash-mounted radio. There were some mechanical teething problems, but the later supercharged 812 Cords

BELOW The De Soto Airflow was launched along with its larger cousin the Chrysler Airflow in 1934. Its streamlining and unibody construction (where major body panels were part of the structure of the car rather than just clothing a chassis) were innovative but ultimately not admired by the general public.

RIGHT A poster advertising Auburn's Boattail Speedster, one of the first American sports cars. It set the standard for the future – large proportions and strong straight-line performance. This Auburn boasted a straight-line speed in excess of 160 kmph (100 mph).

were easily capable of 160 kmph (100 mph) with a 0–97 kmph (0–60 mph) time of around 13 seconds – outstanding performance for a standard road car in the 1930s. Cord-style retractable headlights also featured on an amazing styling concept from Buick in 1938 known as "the Y-Job". With wrap-around bumpers and door handles flush to the bodywork, the Y-Job was a glimpse of things to come, American car designs of the 1950s clearly following its lead.

In 1938 a totally different kind of car was beginning to roll off the production lines in a purpose-built town called Stadt des Kdf-Wagens (now Wolfsburg) in Germany. The revolutionary Volkswagen, later to be known as the Beetle, with its rear-mounted, air-cooled, boxer engine, was at first named the KdF-Wagen. KdF stood for *Kraft durch Freude*, which translates as "strength through joy" and was the name that Adolf Hitler gave to the car. Although it would go on to set worldwide production records over the next 65 years, very few Beetles were actually produced prior to the outbreak of the Second World War.

BELOW The world's first concept car, the Buick Y-Job, seen here with its designer, Harley J Earl. As director of design at General Motors, Earl pioneered the creation of concept cars both as a tool used during the design process and as a marketing device.

Harley Earl (1893–1969)

Few designers have had such a profound influence on the development of the car as did Harley Earl. He laid the foundations by working with his father in their Hollywood coachbuilding business. When it was bought by a local Cadillac dealer, Harley remained as director of the bodyshop but was soon head hunted by General Motors to create what became their Styling Division. Earl was instrumental in introducing annual model changes to drive sales by making old cars obsolete and new cars a more desirable status symbol. He was also responsible for the astounding Buick Y-Job concept (see picture below) and instigated "Project Opel" which became the Chevrolet Corvette.

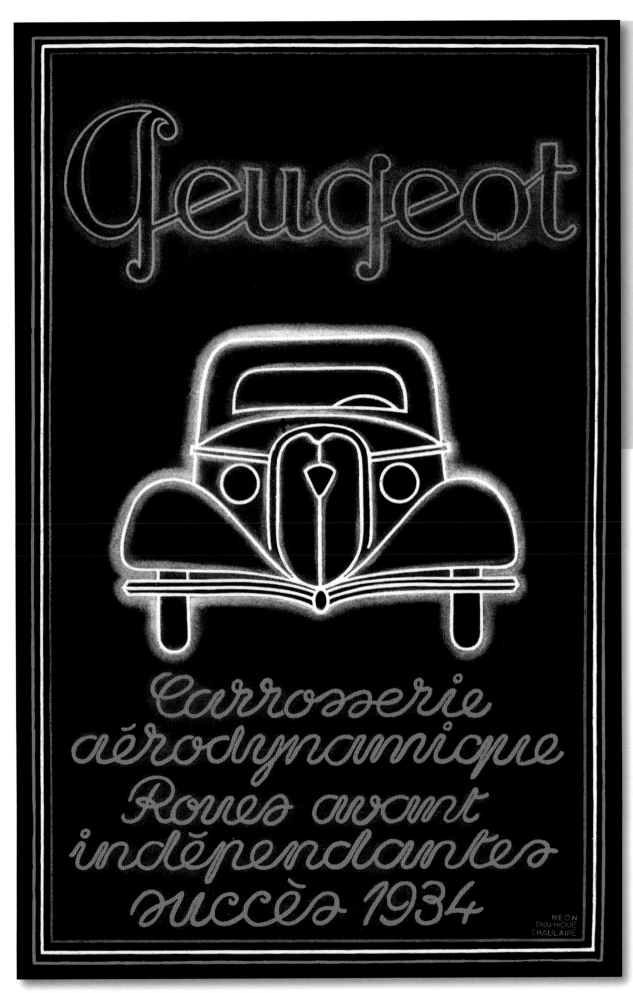

Although neon lights had been used on advertising signs since the 1920s, the neon style of this Peugeot poster looks way ahead of its time for 1934, which is certainly in keeping with the ultra-modern Peugeot. The image is of a Peugeot 401 boasting "aerodynamic bodywork" and "independent front suspension", the French company being the first to offer such a feature as standard on their cars. The 401 was also ahead of the game when the Eclipse model was introduced with a retractable, electric, folding hard-top, a feature that is still found on Peugeots (and a variety of other manufacturers' cars) today. It would be another 20 years before Ford re-invented the automatic folding hard-top in their Skyliner model.

OVERLEAF The Bugatti Type 57 SC Atlantic. Sometimes cited as the most beautiful car ever created, there are only two left in the world. This one is owned by fashion designer Ralph Lauren. The other became the most expensive car to be sold at auction, fetching over $30,000,000 in May 2010.

The Bugatti Queen and the Silver Arrows

The Great Depression that followed the stock market crashes of 1929 saw the demand for new cars plummet and many car makers found themselves in difficulties. Some simply closed down and disappeared. In Germany, where there had been more than 80 car manufacturers at the end of the First World War in 1918, the number dwindled throughout the 1920s, leading some of the survivors to merge with former rivals. The two giants of the German motor industry, Daimler and Benz, had finally merged in 1926 after several years of talks and negotiations.

Another momentous German merger came about in 1932. Horch, who had produced stylish luxury cars, and Audi, a company formed by engineer August Horch (1868–1951) in 1909 after he was forced out of the business bearing his own name following a dispute with his partners, merged with DKW (originally a manufacturer of Dampf-Kraft-Wagen – steam cars) and Wanderer, another quality auto name. As in the giant American corporations, cars continued to be produced under the different brand names, but the umbrella company was now known as Auto Union, representing its four constituent companies with a corporate emblem of four linked rings. It was as Auto Union that the company received backing from Adolf Hitler's government in its "racing for Germany" programme, intended as a morale-booster for a fatigued population and to show everyone that Germany was a world-beater when it came to modern technology. The car they produced was truly revolutionary. Designed by Ferdinand Porsche (see page 31), it had a supercharged V-16 engine mounted behind the driver but in front of the rear wheels. This mid-engined configuration predated the layout of modern Grand Prix cars by more than 25 years. The Auto Union A-type competed in 1934, winning the German, Swiss and Hungarian Grands Prix, but suffered mechanical teething problems that saw other wins slip from its grasp. A slightly modified B-type took to the field in 1935, winning its first Grand Prix in Tunis and taking both first and second

places at Pescara in Italy, where one of the Auto Unions was timed at over 290 kmph (180 mph). The C-type of 1936, however, was the most successful of all. It scored first, second and third finishes at Pescara and in the Swiss Grand Prix, the cars continuing to race unchanged through 1937, with notable wins in Britain at Donington and in the prestigious Vanderbilt Cup race in America.

Competition for the Auto Union came from their German compatriots at Mercedes-Benz, initially with their W25. It is believed that it was the W25 that began the legend of "The Silver Arrows" when it had all of its paint scraped off in order to meet weight restrictions prior to racing at the Nürburgring. It had become traditional for cars to race in national colours, the British adopting green, the Italians racing in red, the French in blue, the Belgians in yellow and the Germans in white, but the success of the W25 and the similarly unpainted Auto Unions led the Germans to change their racing colour to silver. Like the Auto Union cars, development of the W25 was subsidized by the German government and the car saw several successes in the 1934 season before gaining driver Rudolf Caracciola (see page 47) the European Championship title in 1935.

Italian ace Tazio Nuvolari (1892–1953) won the German Grand Prix for Scuderia Ferrari in 1935 in his Alfa Romeo Tipo B but he was chased home by

Mercedes W25s and Auto Unions in the following eight positions. Except for Nuvolari's solitary Grand Prix win, German cars would go on to win every other European Championship race between 1935 and 1939. For the 1937 season, the Mercedes W25 was superseded by the W125, which was faster and more powerful. Its 5.6-litre, eight-cylinder engine could produce 637 horsepower and propel the silver racer to over 306 kmph (190 mph). Hermann Lang (1901–1976) drove the car to victory on its first outing in Tunis while a string of successes once more made Caracciola European Champion. Successive "Silver Arrow" Mercedes-Benz racers were developed to meet qualification specifications for Grand Prix events right up to the outbreak of the Second World War, with Alfa Romeo's Tipo 158 one of the few cars able to compete with the mighty Germans.

ABOVE Germany achieved a historic 1-2 at the Pau Grand Prix in 1939 when Hermann Lang won in his Mercedes W125 with Manfred von Brauchitsch coming second in an identical car.

OPPOSITE ABOVE German racing driver Bernd Rosemeyer in the Auto Union Type C, competing in a hill climb in Germany in 1936.

OPPOSITE BELOW The fiery Italian Luigi Fagioli, reputed once to have started a brawl with rival Rudolf Caracciola, competing in a Mercedes-Benz W25.

While the winning teams attracted the star drivers, there were also sparkles of glamour to be found elsewhere on the racetrack. The woman who became known as "The Queen of Speed" was carving a name for herself in the macho world of motor racing. Mariette Hélène Delangle (1900–1984) was the daughter of a postman and left home at the age of 16 to work in the music halls of Paris. Under the name Hélène Nice, later shortened to Hellé Nice, she became an exotic dancer and model, and was so successful that she toured Europe with her act, making enough money to buy a house and her own yacht. The athletic Hellé loved skiing but an accident on the slopes put an end to her dancing career, prompting her to take an active interest in motor racing. She won an all-female Grand Prix at Montlhéry in 1929 and also toured the United States racing Millers. Hellé was associated with several members of prominent families throughout Europe and, helped by her lover Philippe de Rothschild (1902–1988), who had raced for Bugatti and introduced her to Ettore Bugatti (see chapter 5), she raced a Bugatti Type 35C in Grand Prix events in 1931, competing against the men. Although Hellé never actually won a major Grand Prix, she regularly finished ahead of some of the biggest names in the sport, racing against drivers such as Nuvolari, Bernd Rosemeyer (1909–1938), Caracciola and Louis Chiron (1899–1979). Then, while lying in second place during the 1936 Sao Paulo Grand Prix in Brazil, she crashed into a straw bale at over 160 kmph (100 mph), apparently trying to avoid spectators. The Alfa Romeo she was driving cartwheeled into the crowd, killing four and causing dozens of injuries. Hellé was flung from the vehicle, landing on a soldier. The impact killed the soldier, but he undoubtedly saved Hellé's life. She spent two months in hospital recovering from her injuries.

Hellé spent the next three years trying to break back into top-class racing, until the Second World War brought racing in Europe to a halt. With the Germans occupying France, she moved to a villa on the south coast in 1943, spending the rest of the war there. In 1949, at a function to mark the resumption of motor racing after the war, Louis Chiron publicly accused Hellé of having been a Gestapo collaborator. No evidence has been found to support his claim but Hellé was shunned thereafter. Her money ran out and she spent the final years of her life in poverty in Nice, where she died in 1984.

PREVIOUS PAGES This 1937 Mercedes Benz W125 won the Tripoli Grand Prix in 1937, with Hermann Lang driving. The W125 is considered a development of the W25.

OPPOSITE Guiseppe Farina in his Alfa Romeo Tipo 158 at the Tripoli Grand Prix in 1939. Although forced to retire with an overheating engine, he won at Tripoli the following year, the last time the Grand Prix was held at the city's Autodromo di Mehalla.

Dick Seaman (1913–1939)

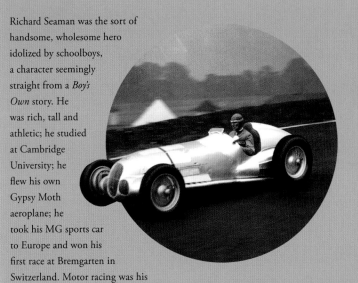

Richard Seaman was the sort of handsome, wholesome hero idolized by schoolboys, a character seemingly straight from a *Boy's Own* story. He was rich, tall and athletic; he studied at Cambridge University; he flew his own Gypsy Moth aeroplane; he took his MG sports car to Europe and won his first race at Bremgarten in Switzerland. Motor racing was his passion and Seaman wanted to compete with the best. In 1936, he won the Grand Prix at Donington and was invited to join the Mercedes-Benz Silver Arrows. He was treated like a Hollywood star by the European press, especially when he married Erica Popp, the beautiful, aristocratic daughter of the General Director of BMW. In 1938 he won the German Grand Prix and was photographed reluctantly giving the Nazi salute on the winners' podium (the English football team had done the same thing earlier in the year when playing Germany). With war looming, Seaman faced an awkward choice about returning to Britain but, sadly, it was a decision he never had to make. He crashed in the rain while leading the Belgian Grand Prix in June 1939 and died as a result of his injuries.

BELOW The glamorous Hellé Nice with her Alfa Romeo Monza 8C prior to the start of the Grand Prix du Comminges in France in 1934.

Surviving the War Years

Long before war was declared in 1939, the motor industries in the countries most likely to become embroiled in the conflict began preparing themselves for war production. In Britain, the government belatedly embarked on a re-armament programme to put the armed forces on a war footing and part of this process involved setting up "shadow factories" – production facilities that could carry on working should factories well known to the enemy be bombed and put out of action.

Car manufacturers such as Rover, who had been building cars in Coventry since 1904, suddenly found themselves running factories producing, in Rover's case, not cars but aero engines and airframes. Rover also became involved in the development of the gas turbine engine with Frank Whittle (1907–1996).

The standard cars produced by motor manufacturers were requisitioned for military use, becoming staff cars or being fed into military transport pools. There was little or no market for ordinary cars among the general public because fuel quickly became so heavily rationed that it was virtually unobtainable to all but those deemed "essential users", such as doctors or police officers. Motoring for pleasure was a pastime that had to wait until the war was over. MG, whose sports cars had covered themselves in glory at Brooklands and had broken speed records throughout the 1930s, were reduced to producing pots and pans or refurbishing old military trucks for a time at their Abingdon plant until they, too, began producing aircraft and then tanks. Other British manufacturers were required to produce stripped-down versions of their own vehicles specifically for military use. These cars, generally with a canvas-covered rear load space instead of rear seats, were known as "Tillys", short for Car, Light Utility 4x2 (not to be confused with the Willys Jeep, see page 66), and many thousands were produced by Austin, Hillman, Morris and Standard.

For American manufacturers who had already established footholds in Europe, the war became something of an embarrassment in that, especially prior to America entering the war in 1941, companies like Ford and GM were making money producing vehicles for both sides. Ford's largest European plant was at Dagenham in England, where they built the tracked Universal or "Bren" carrier as well as other

RIGHT Race sequences for the 1950 movie *To Please A Lady,* in which Clark Gable played a maverick racing driver, were shot using racing cars at Indianapolis, but for the daily commute to film less frantic scenes at MGM's Hollywood studios, Gable made do with his Jaguar XK120.

BELOW LEFT The prototype Land Rover was originally intended as an agricultural vehicle capable of drawing a plough. For accurate ploughing, the vehicle was given a central steering wheel, just like a tractor.

ABOVE The Ferrari 125S was the first car properly to bear the Ferrari name. A racing sports car that made its debut at the Piacenza racing circuit in May 1947, only two were ever built.

engines and vehicles, while in Manchester Ford's original British factory produced Rolls-Royce Merlin engines for the Lancaster aircraft that flew to Germany to bomb Cologne where Ford had its German factory! GM were in a similar position, having bought British manufacturer Vauxhall in 1925 and Opel in 1929. Churchill tanks made by Vauxhall attacked columns of Opel supply trucks in the deserts of North Africa. The situation became even more ludicrous when both companies began making vehicles and aircraft for the US military, although by then they had lost most of their control of their European operations.

The drive towards recovery after 1945 saw the appearance of a number of radical new cars. The Porsche Type 60, better known as the Volkswagen Beetle (see page 50), had never gone into full production before the war came along and its chassis were used for military vehicles. In 1945, the VW factory was supposed to be taken apart and shipped to Britain, but no British manufacturer was interested in taking it on. To solve their own transport problems and help to kick-start the local economy, therefore, the British Army took over the Wolfsburg plant and began producing the car that would become a legend.

Hints at the shape of things to come were being whispered with vestigial fins on the Harley Earl and Frank Hershey-designed Cadillac for 1948, while the grand old aristocrat of the motoring world, Rolls-Royce, began taking a modern approach by supplying cars fully fitted with bodywork. A more rugged approach was taken with a new car from Rover in 1948. Intended as a stop-gap to keep their factory in production until a better option became available, the Land Rover was inspired by the Willys Jeep and intended for agricultural work. Its four-wheel drive and robust bodywork were soon found to be ideal for farming and military applications,

Sir William Lyons (1901–85)

Tinkering with old motorcycles and building sidecars as a hobby turned into a serious enterprise when William Lyons and his next-door neighbour William Walmsley (b. 1892) borrowed £500 from their fathers to go into business together. Blackpool-born Lyons had worked as an apprentice engineer at Crossley Motors in Manchester and sold cars for a Sunbeam dealership before establishing his own business with Walmsley in 1922. They manufactured streamlined sidecars, but by 1927 had branched out into making a coach-built saloon car – the Austin Swallow. Lyons had a fine eye for line and form, and although he had no formal training as a designer, produced the rakish SS1 car in 1931, changing the company name to SS Cars. The association with the Nazis led to him adopt the name Jaguar instead after the war. Walmsley having left the company in 1933, Lyons led Jaguar to become a hugely respected marque, producing saloon cars of unequalled refinement and sports cars that stunned the motoring world.

although later versions of the car were to be more luxurious. Like the Beetle, the Land Rover was set to become a household name. A far rarer legend was also created in 1948 when Jaguar, a company that had originally produced motorcycle sidecars and re-bodied Austin Sevens (see box feature), unveiled its stunning XK120 sports car at the London Motor Show. The low-slung two-seater cost £998, a fraction of the price of any other road car that could hope to match its shattering performance. The "120" in its name indicated the car's top speed and to prove it Jaguar staged a demonstration for invited journalists on the long, straight stretch of motorway at Jabbeke in Belgium. The car did not do 193 kmph (120 mph) – it reached just over 209 kmph (130 mph).

Another sports car that first appeared in 1948 and which established a name that would become synonymous with desirable motor cars was the Porsche 356. Initially based largely on Volkswagen parts, the 356 was largely the brainchild of Ferdinand Porsche's son, "Ferry" (1909–1998), and although it wasn't as fast as the new Jaguar, its handling was widely praised. Various versions of the 356 remained in production for the next 17 years. Two more cars set to enjoy seriously long production runs also debuted in 1948. The Morris Minor was a thoroughly modern car for the economically minded motorist. The little car could accommodate four adult passengers and could make 103 kmph (64 mph), yet its fuel consumption was as low as 14 km per litre (40 miles per gallon) and it cost under £400. The Minor was to remain in production as a four-door, estate, convertible or commercial vehicle until 1971. The second car was from Citroën, who had produced the amazing front-wheel drive Traction Avant in 1934. They offered another front-wheel drive car for 1948 – the 2CV. This economy car had many innovative features including a four-speed gearbox when many other cars still had only three. Its tiny, two-cylinder, air-cooled engine had a very distinctive sound and its bodywork looked neither streamlined nor modern in any way. Motoring journalists could not invent enough terms of abuse for the car's sloth-like performance, but the public loved its simplicity and its meagre running costs. It could easily achieve 17.5 km per litre (50 miles per gallon). Its popularity kept the quirky 2CV in production in various forms until 1990.

OPPOSITE AND PREVIOUS PAGE There is a strong family resemblance between Ferdinand Porsche's 356, which first appeared in 1948, and his pre-war design for what became known as the Volkswagen Beetle.

BELOW The Citroën 2CV was slow, noisy and draughty, and wallowed around corners as though the wheels and body were determined to take different routes... but people loved it. It was basic, but quite cute and, best of all, it could do around 80 km (50 miles) to the gallon.

Icons of War

It was the car they said couldn't be built. No less than 135 motor manufacturers in the United States were asked to make a new small truck for the United States Army. Only three agreed to try. The problem was that the military appeared to be asking for the impossible. The truck had to have a wheelbase of 190 cm (75 inches), although that specification was later extended to 203 cm (80 inches), and a track of 119 cm (47 inches), but be big enough to carry at least three fully-equipped soldiers and a .30 calibre machine gun. Unladen, the vehicle was to weigh no more than 590 kg (1,300 lb), to allow for easy manhandling, and it had to have four-wheel drive. It needed to be capable of climbing a 45° slope, of descending a 35° slope and of wading through water 46 cm (18 inches) deep.

The specification was issued in 1940 when war was already raging in Europe and the army needed to update its ageing vehicle fleet. If it was to be ready to go to war, the army needed transport, and it demanded that manufacturers competing for the new order have a prototype ready in 49 days with 70 vehicles ready to roll on test in 75 days.

The companies who thought they could produce the goods were Ford, Willys Overland and American Bantam. Bantam had previously made Austin Sevens under licence but were now suffering financial problems. They persuaded engineer Karl Probst (see box feature page 68) to design the vehicle and he did so in just three days, allowing Bantam, under his direction, to prepare and present their prototype ahead of Ford and Willys. When Bantam's "Blitz Buggy" was put through its paces at an army test centre in Maryland, designers from Ford and Willys were there to watch. The army even gave them copies of the blueprints and sent them away to come up with their best effort. The Willys "Quad" and the Ford "Pigmy" were the results and they were tested along with a revised Bantam model. The Willys car had the most powerful engine but was struggling to come in under the revised overall weight limit of 980 kg (2,160 lb) and the others also each had their strengths and failings.

Eventually, 1,500 of each were ordered for extensive testing by the units that would ultimately be expected to take them to war. Both the Ford and the Willys vehicles borrowed heavily from the Bantam, but the authorities were unconvinced that Bantam would be able to produce the car in the quantities they would need and to the timetable they would have to impose. Willys finally got the order for 16,000 vehicles, each one costing around US$740, but they were told to include the best of the Ford features on their vehicle. The finished item, therefore, turned out to be an amalgamation of all three manufacturers' ideas. And the name? Ford had designated their final version the "GP", which does not, as some have assumed, stand for General Purpose. The G was for "government" and the P apparently identified the wheelbase. Gee Pee became "Jeep", although the acronym GP was used for General Purpose in the military, so the name may well have some of its roots there, too. While Willys built more than 335,530 Jeeps during the Second World War, the army needed Ford's production capacity to keep up with demand and Ford contributed almost 280,000 units.

The Jeep was a huge success for the Allies, but the Germans had their own utility vehicle, specially designed for them by Ferdinand Porsche. The Kübelwagen used the chassis and engine from the Volkswagen Beetle with lightweight body panels providing enough room for four occupants. The flat-four "boxer" engine (so called because the pistons move horizontally, pushing the crankshaft from either side as though they are boxing with each other) was at the rear and could push the Kübelwagen to 80 kmph (50 mph). Because it was air-cooled, the engine didn't have the disadvantage of being disabled by gunfire damaging the radiator and because it was mounted over the rear wheels, it gave the German car an off-road performance almost as good as that of the Jeep. More than 50,000 Kübelwagens were built

OPPOSITE The Jeep was used as a scout car armed with heavy machine guns; as general transport for all ranks; as an ambulance; and in a multitude of other roles including, as seen here, to help roll agricultural land in England.

ABOVE German troops in a VW Schwimmwagen during the Battle of the Bulge in 1944.

BELOW The Kübelwagen, manufactured using the engine and chassis designed for the VW Beetle, had the engine mounted over the rear wheels, giving it good traction on soft ground.

Karl Probst (1883–1963)

Born in the small town of Point Pleasant in West Virginia, Karl Probst will forever be associated with another small town – Butler in Pennsylvania, where he worked for the American Bantam Car Company.

After graduating from Ohio State University in 1906, Probst worked for a number of different car companies such as Chalmers, Peerless and Reo, having been fascinated with "horseless carriages" since he was a boy. He established himself as a freelance or consultant design engineer and it was in this capacity that he worked for Bantam. When he was asked to design a utility vehicle for the company at short notice, Probst fully understood that the perilous state of Bantam's finances meant that he might never be paid for his work, yet he completed the job and even drove the prototype, along with Bantam's chief engineer, for two days to reach the army's proving grounds on time. Although Bantam did not, ultimately, build the Jeep, Karl Probst showed that it could be done and is justly known as the "father of the Jeep".

during the Second World War, along with 15,000 of its amphibious cousin, the Schwimmwagen. The Schwimmwagen was not a craft in which you could put to sea, but it was ideal for crossing rivers. Its body was a waterproof tub as opposed to the Kübelwagen's flat panels and a propeller could be lowered at the rear, driven directly from the crankshaft. The vehicle's wheels could also help it "swim" through the water, with four-wheel drive available in first gear to help it climb up or down muddy river banks.

Military vehicles are all very well for soldiers in the field, but military commanders need to be seen in something that better fitted their exalted status. Adolf Hitler (1889–1945) was pictured in a variety of the finest Mercedes vehicles. Some, like the official armoured Mercedes 540 cars, were elegant yet practical transport for a paranoid dictator. One of Hitler's 540s was known as the "Swabian Colossus" because its armour weighed so much, and adapting the car was said to have cost £40,000 – equivalent to at least £1.5 million nowadays. Hitler was also seen in a Mercedes G4 limousine. The six-wheeled monster was less limo and more truck – with power to four wheels at the rear that made it ideal for reviewing troops on manoeuvres in the countryside but a poor getaway car as its 5.4-litre engine could only drag it along at about 65 kmph (40 mph).

Without doubt the most impressive of Hitler's cars was the Mercedes 770. Introduced in 1930, the 770 was also known as the Großer Mercedes and only around 200 examples were built throughout its 13-year production run. The type used by Hitler was the Series 1, produced up to 1938. It was the most expensive Mercedes built up to that point and how much you paid for it really just depended on how much you wanted to spend. It had a 7.7-litre engine with a supercharger that could be engaged by the driver, a six-speed gearbox, power-assisted brakes and a top speed of around 160 kmph (100 mph). Emperor Hirohito of Japan had several 770s but it was Hitler who will forever be associated with the car, despite the fact that he never actually learned to drive.

RIGHT The amphibious vehicle from Volkswagen on a muddy road on the eastern front.

The Fin's the Thing

Fuel rationing in America during the Second World War had been far less restrictive than in the UK, with the American government more worried about running out of tyres than about petrol shortages. Petrol rationing ended in the US in 1945 but in Britain it continued until 1950 (and was re-introduced for a short while during the Suez Crisis in 1956), when the dawn of a new decade brought with it some sensational new car designs. The motoring public was certainly ready to get back on the road.

At the 1950 Paris Auto Show, Ferrari displayed its new 340 America. Enzo Ferrari (see box feature page 44) had parted company with Alfa Romeo in 1937 and had established his own racing team, building two cars to compete in the 1940 Mille Miglia. By 1947 Ferrari was making road cars, basically road-legal versions of his Grand Prix cars, with sales helping to fund the racing team. Only two examples of the first car, the 1947 Ferrari 125 S, were actually built, making the Ferrari a truly exclusive marque. The Ferrari 340 America in 1950 would have a production run of just 23 cars, with the sensational looks and performance of the new Ferrari making the America series highly desirable for more than just their exclusivity. These were "bespoke" sports cars with the factory supplying the rolling chassis and engine ready for a design house to create the bodywork. The 26 375MM Americas produced in 1953 were clothed either by Ghia, Pinin Farina, Vignale or, in the case of one particular car, Scaglietti. The Scaglietti car was known as the 375

ABOVE When it came to fins, the Cadillac Eldorado Biarritz was hard to beat but beneath its outrageous styling lay a wealth of features still regarded as luxuries on cars more than 50 years later.

OPPOSITE The Ferrari 250 GT California Spyder is a worthy contender for the crown for The Most Beautiful Car Ever Made.

BELOW Ford's Thunderbird grew bigger every year, but so did its sales. This 1957 model sold 30 per cent more than the launch model two years before.

America "Ingrid Bergman Coupé" as it was commissioned by film director Roberto Rossellini (1906–1977) for his then wife Ingrid Bergman (1915–1982).

Along with the America series, Ferrari also produced what was widely regarded as the most versatile of all its cars, the 250 GT series. These cars began to appear in 1953 and became available in various guises, as GT or "Gran Turismo" sports cars capable of covering huge distances at great speed, as sports racing cars intended for use on the track or as a cross between the two – road cars that could also be used on the race track. The 250 GT California Spyder is one of the most beautiful cars ever made, while closed coupé versions of the 250 GT were incredibly fast, the 3-litre V-12 engine propelling the car from standstill to 97 kmph (60 mph) in a little over six seconds, with a top speed of more than 240 kmph (150 mph).

While European styling tended to favour smooth lines and flowing curves, American designers were indulging in far more flamboyant experiments with fins and other protrusions. Ferrari joined the party with the 410 Superamerica at the 1956 Paris Auto Show, but for the most outrageous jet-aircraft-inspired fins, air scoops and missile-like adornments, it was difficult to beat the 1957 Plymouth Fury or Imperial Crown… unless you bought a 1959 Cadillac Eldorado Biarritz – the queen of fin chic. But these gleaming chrome monsters (the Eldorado Biarritz was almost 5.8 m/19 ft long and 1.9 m/6 ft 8 inches wide) came packed with the latest automotive technology. Car radios had first been introduced in the 1920s and grew in popularity through the 1930s but the Cadillac had the newest push-button radio, air conditioning, electric door locks, power windows, power seats, cruise control, automatically dimming headlights, tinted glass, power-assisted steering, power-assisted brakes and all sorts of other goodies. Cadillac owners did not have to struggle raising or lowering the soft top, because the car did that for you. The electric motors stowed the roof in a well behind the rear seats, clipping a metal cover in place to preserve the car's stylish lines. Other cars, such as the 1958 Lincoln Continental, had power soft tops, but few had gone as far as Ford with its 1957 Fairlane 500 Skyliner and fitted a steel roof that could retract into the trunk. The Skyliner wasn't hugely popular but the retractable hard top was an idea that would be revisited by several manufacturers half a century later.

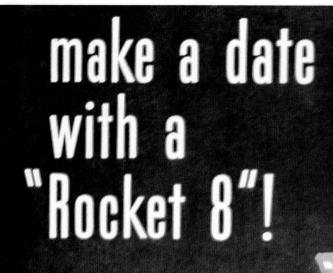

make a date with a "Rocket 8"!

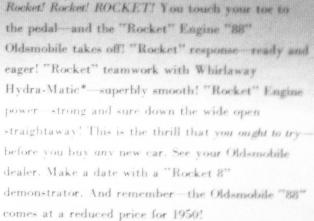

Rocket! Rocket! ROCKET! You touch your toe to the pedal—and the "Rocket" Engine "88" Oldsmobile takes off! "Rocket" response—ready and eager! "Rocket" teamwork with Whirlaway Hydra-Matic*—superbly smooth! "Rocket" Engine power—strong and sure down the wide open straightaway! This is the thrill that *you ought to try*—before you buy *any* new car. See your Oldsmobile dealer. Make a date with a "Rocket 8" demonstrator. And remember—the Oldsmobile "88" comes at a reduced price for 1950!

"88"

*Whirlaway Hydra-Matic Drive, at reduced price, now optional on all Oldsmobile models.

A GENERAL MOTORS VALUE

Rocket Ahead with OLDSMOBILE

PREVIOUS PAGES Less than three dozen Ferrari 410 Superamerica models were built between 1955 and 1959. Each was different, with custom-built bodywork, this one by Ghia of Turin.

1950 Oldsmobile Poster

"Make a date with a Rocket 8!" is how the Oldsmobile advertising line ran when they began promoting the first incarnation of the Oldsmobile 88. The 88 was launched in 1949, slotting into the range between the company's small "76" model and the larger, more luxurious "98" model. The 88 was largely based on the 76 but instead of the small cars 6 cylinder engine, it had the new V8 "Rocket" engine originally intended for the 98. The Rocket was Oldsmobile's first post-war, high-performance V8 engine and dropping it into the lightweight 88 gave the car a top speed in excess of 161 kmph (100 mph). Along with what Oldsmobile described as "Futuramic styling" which, for 1950, meant a one-piece windscreen as well as the rocket ornament on the bonnet, the car's performance made it the first of the "muscle car" breed.

"Safety Fast!" Poster

"Safety Fast!" was the slogan that the MG Car Company adopted in the late 1930s and continued to use well beyond 1953, when the MG TF pictured on the poster first appeared. The TF was a development the TD, which in turn was a development of the TC and the T-type, a line of traditional, two-seat sports cars that stretched back to 1936. By the time the TF was in production, MG had been sucked into the motor industry's conglomerate chaos, becoming part of Morris Motors in 1935, then BMC (British Motor Corporation) in 1952, British Motor Holdings in 1966 and the British Leyland Motor Corporation (BLMC) in 1968. In 1975, the part-nationalised BLMC became BL and in 1980 the decline in the British Motor industry saw the MG name disappear completely when the last of its manufacturing facilities were shut down. Revived in 1982 as a badge on sports versions of Austin Rover saloons, a new MG emerged in 1995 in the shape of the mid-engined MG F two-seater. Production ceased in 2005 when the Rover Group went under, but restarted in China in 2007 when the Nanjing Automobile Group acquired the rights to the MG brand, introducing the all-new MG6 GT in 2011.

OPPOSITE Faster than the BMW 507 and less than a third of the price, the fibreglass-bodied Chevrolet Corvette boasted supercar performance.

ABOVE The BMW 507 is one of the coolest cars of all time, partly due to the fact that Elvis Presley drove one when he was stationed in Germany between 1958 and 1960.

Alfa Romeo Giulietta

Alfa Romeo introduced the delightful Giulietta in 1954 and it became such a success that it remained in production in various guises for more than ten years. The name was revived for a boxy, four-door Alfa saloon in 1977 and again in 2010 for the latest Giulietta. The original may not have had the performance of the new car (0-60mph took twice as long as the fastest modern Giulietta's 6.8 seconds) but it handled well for its day and its spirited 1290cc engine revved freely enough to make the Giulietta a joy to drive. The little coupe was designed by the Bertone styling house and when it came time to add

a convertible to the Giulietta range, they submitted a couple of concepts, although the final car was the work of Pinin Farina (at that time still two words, not Pininfarina as it is today). They produced a far sleeker body with a remodelled front grille and a soft top that stowed neatly away beneath a panel behind the driver and passenger, giving a clear, uncluttered rear deck. The convertible was first shown to the public as a prototype at the 1955 motor show in Paris and was launched as a production model at the Turin motor show in April the following year. The production convertible was designated model 750 D and these drawings show dimensions and design details.

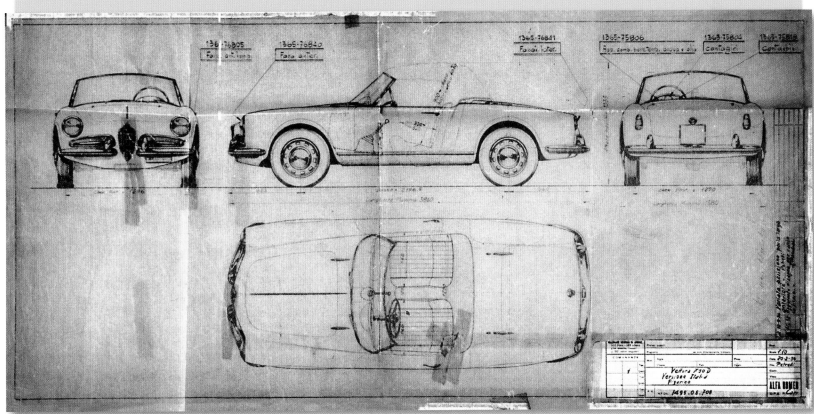

THE FLEETWOOD SIXTY SPECIAL

A NEW REALM OF MOTORING MAJESTY!

THE 1959 *Cadillac*

By appointment to the world's most discriminating motorists!

THE ELDORADO BIARRITZ

A single glance tells you, beyond any question, *that these are the newest and most magnificent Cadillac cars ever created.* Dazzling in their beauty, enchanting in their grace and elegance, and inspiring in their Fleetwood luxury and decor—they introduce a new realm of motoring majesty. And a single journey at the wheel will reveal still another unquestionable fact—*that these are the finest performing Cadillacs ever produced.* With a spectacular new engine, with a smoother, more responsive Hydra-Matic drive, and with improved qualities of ride and handling, they provide a totally new sense of mastery over time and distance. This brilliant new Cadillac beauty and this marvelous new Cadillac performance are offered in thirteen individual body styles. To see and to drive any of them is to acknowledge Cadillac a new measure of automotive supremacy. Your dealer invites you to do both at your first opportunity. CADILLAC MOTOR CAR DIVISION · GENERAL MOTORS CORPORATION

THE SIXTY-TWO COUPE

1959 Cadillac Advertisement

The 1959 Cadillac range displayed all of the glorious excess associated with the jet-age styling, including outrageous fins, "jet thruster" rear styling, lights set in pod clusters and streams of sparkling chrome. Pride of place in this ad is given to the Fleetwood Sixty Special. The "Sixty Special" designation had been used by Cadillac since 1938 to identify a superior model loaded with more equipment and benefiting from extra styling touches. The 1959 incarnation was no exception, noticeable differences between this and the other models being the dummy air scoops that stretched from the middle of the rear door back into the rear wing, and the high-level rear light clusters which were chrome on the Sixty Special but the same colour as the rest of the bodywork on the Eldorado and Sixty-Two Coupe. The Fleetwood badge was also a mark of quality, Fleetwood having been a coach-building company based in the town of Fleetwood, Pennsylvania, that supplied bodywork not only for Cadillac but also for owners of other prestigious marques such as Rolls Royce, Mercedes-Benz and Duesenberg. The company was bought out and eventually became part of General Motors in Detroit in 1931.

Sir Alec Issigonis (1906–1988)

Alexander Arnold Constantine Issigonis was born in Smyrna (now Izmir) in Turkey. His grandfather was Greek but took up British nationality after working as an engineer for a British-run railway company in Smyrna – thanks to this British nationality the Issigonis family was evacuated to Malta when a fire engulfed Smyrna in 1922. Issigonis subsequently moved to the UK to study engineering. He worked for the Humber car company and Austin while racing modified Austin Sevens at events in the UK. By 1936 he was working for Morris and during the Second World War he was involved in a number of new projects, which included a design for a car code-named "Mosquito". This would become the Morris Minor in 1948. Following a brief spell with luxury car maker Alvis, Issigonis rejoined Austin and Morris, the companies having merged to become BMC in 1955. In August 1959 the Morris Mini Minor, also called the Austin Seven but better known simply as the Mini, was launched and it is for designing this car that Issigonis will always be remembered.

OPPOSITE The Corvette could not match the performance of the Mercedes 300 SL, even if the German car's "gullwing" doors couldn't actually make it fly.

Two legends of the American motor industry were born in the 1950s when Chevrolet launched its Corvette late in 1953 and Ford responded with the Thunderbird the following year. The Corvette, with its fibreglass body, was America's first mass-produced sports car but initially it was not a huge success and when Ford's Thunderbird came along it outsold the GM car 23 to 1 in its first year. The Thunderbird, however, was destined to grow bigger and bulkier, while the Corvette's styling remained unashamedly European in its appearance and, especially when it received a fuel-injected, 4.6-litre V-8 engine in 1957, it had the performance to match. The Corvette could reach 97 kmph (60 mph) in around seven seconds and had a top speed of 193 kmph (120 mph). That was more than a match for the Thunderbird, although the Ford still sold three times as many in 1957.

The Corvette also gave its European rivals a run for their money. In 1955 BMW showed its 507 sports car at the Frankfurt Motor Show and, as it was intended for the American market, at the Waldorf-Astoria Hotel in New York. When compared to the Corvette, however, the 507 was not as quick off the mark and cost around US$10,000. The Corvette was priced at just US$3,000. Only 252 507s were ever built. There was another German car that could easily match the Corvette's performance, and without its bodywork rattling, warping

and leaking – common problems with the early Corvette fibreglass. The Mercedes-Benz 300 SL "Gullwing", so called because its doors opened upwards to look something like the wings of a bird, was a race-bred sports car that could reach 258 kmph (160 mph). Launched in 1954 at the New York Motor Show, the 300 SL had a 3-litre engine and was one of the first road cars to use fuel injection rather than carburettors. It was, at that time, the fastest car on the road. Like the BMW 507, however, its advanced German technology came at a price – US$11,000.

It may not have had the luxury of the American cars or the performance of the Europeans, but Britain's Mini became a motoring icon nevertheless when it went on sale in 1959. The little car designed by Sir Alec Issigonis (see box feature page 78) had just a tiny 850-cc engine and equipment levels were kept to an absolute minimum to make the Mini an affordable, economical city car. There were no door handles inside, for example, just wires with which to pull the doors closed. There were sliding widows to save space and cost, exterior welding and door hinges to make production cheaper and very few creature comforts – not even a radio. The top speed was 116 kmph (72 mph) but there was room for four adults and a surprising amount of luggage – all for £496, equivalent to less than US$1,500. The Mini was an instant hit. (See also page 88.)

The Top Cats

Motorsport was brought to the masses in a way that had never really happened before when televisions began to appear in every home during the 1950s. The BBC had broadcast its first motor race as long ago as 1937 when the dashing B Bira, otherwise known as Prince Birabongse Bhanudej Bhanubandh of Siam (1914–1985), won the International Imperial Trophy Race at London's now defunct Crystal Palace circuit in his ERA (English Racing Automobile) R2B. Motor racing had been shown on cinema newsreels, of course, and there was extensive newspaper coverage, but television brought the danger and the glamour into the living room, quite literally turning the stars of motor racing into household names.

Juan Manuel Fangio (1911–1995) began his motor racing career in his native Argentina in 1934 and would by today's standards be far too old at 38 to be competing in Formula 1. Yet he had shown his worth by winning a clutch of Grands Prix in 1949 in his Maserati and, for the new Formula 1 Drivers' World Championship in 1950, he was recruited by Alfa Romeo to drive their 159 Alfetta. He narrowly lost the first World Championship to Guiseppe Farina (see below), also driving for Alfa

Romeo, but took the title in 1951. Alfa Romeo having withdrawn from Formula 1, Fangio returned to Maserati, sustaining serious injuries in a crash at Monza that entailed many months of recovery at home in Argentina. By 1953 he was back racing with Maserati, finishing second in the Championship and the following year he drove for both Maserati and, later, Mercedes, winning six out of the eight World Championship events to regain his title. In 1955 he took the title driving for Mercedes and in 1956 he moved to Ferrari, winning a further world

title. For the 1957 season, Fangio, now 46 years old, was back in a Maserati, who were still fielding the 250 F racer that he had driven in 1954. He won in Argentina, Monaco and France before battling his way past the Ferrari of Mike Hawthorn (see below) in an epic race at the Nürburgring to take his fifth World Championship title. Fangio retired the following year, having won an amazing 24 Grands Prix from 51 starts.

Fangio dominated the Drivers' World Championship throughout the 1950s, but the first World Championship was won by his teammate Giuseppe "Nino" Farina (1906–1966). Farina was born in Turin, Italy, and grew up with motor cars in his blood, his father an engineer and his uncle "Pinin" Farina a respected coachbuilder. Farina first found success with his racing career in the 1930s and, like Fangio, was a little long in the tooth for a racing driver by the time he became World Champion with Alfa Romeo at the age of 44 in 1950. Moving to Ferrari in 1952, Farina continued to be competitive but suffered a number of injuries in accidents. Having retired in 1957, he was killed in a road accident while driving to watch the 1966 French Grand Prix.

ABOVE Giuseppe Farina in his Alfa Romeo 158 at Silverstone in 1950. He came second, with Juan Manuel Fangio winning, Luigi Fagioli in a 158 coming third and Reg Parnell finishing fourth, also in a 158.

OPPOSITE One of the most charismatic World Champions, Argentinian Juan Manuel Fangio almost lost his life when he crashed his Maserati at Monza in 1952.

The son of Alfa Romeo star Antonio Ascari (see page 43), Alberto Ascari (1918–1955) was Farina's teammate, racing the Ferrari Tipo 500 in 1952 and 1953 when Ascari's unique achievement was to become the only Italian driver to win two World Championships driving the quintessentially Italian racing car, Ferrari. In 1954, Ascari drove for Maserati, although he managed one more race for Ferrari the same year before joining Scuderia Lancia. At the 1955 Monaco Grand Prix he gained the distinction of being one of only two drivers (both survived) to take their cars for a swim in Monaco Harbour. Sadly, Ascari's luck was to run out later that year when he died in a crash at Monza. He was laid to rest alongside his father at the Cimitero Monumentale in Milan.

26 Jan 48

development of SS100

4 cyl. twin ohc.
2 SU carb. 2 litre?
Jaguar

with all enclosed
alloy body of very
strong construction
weighing less than
200 lb?

car appears too
stubby
tail good
wings good
rad. bad.
cockpit unprotected
2 bucket seats –
lots of gear box in cockpit.

disc wheels

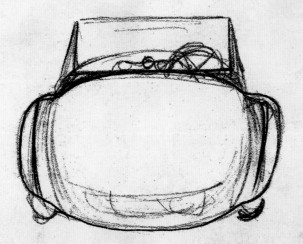

hope to be ready for
1948 Earls Court

ABOVE Stirling Moss on his way to winning the Monaco Grand Prix in 1961, driving the Lotus 18 in which he almost died at Goodwood the following year.

OVERLEAF The D-Type Jaguar, with the distinctive fin that helped to stop it drifting at speeds of up to 306 kmph (190 mph), winning at Le Mans in 1955.

Jaguar XK120 Sketch

This early sketch of the Jaguar XK120 is marked "development of SS100", the SS 100 being Jaguar's pre-war sports car. The SS100, however, did not have headlights set into the bodywork and front wings that were integral to the bodywork. This "development of the SS100" clearly takes some of its styling cues from the 1938 Bugatti Atlantic and the 1940 BMW 328 "Mille Miglia". The first XK120s, rather more streamlined and refined than this sketch, would bear a strong resemblance to the BMW when the car was launched, just nine months after this preliminary sketch was made, at the Earl's Court Motor Show in October 1948. It was then that the new Jaguar Super Sports became the XK120. Gone was the four cylinder, 2 litre engine noted on this sketch, although it was this version of Jaguar's XK engine that powered Lieutenant Colonel Gardner's streamlined MG to a world record 283 kmph (176 mph) over a 0.6 mile (1 km) course in September 1948. The 2 litre caused too much noise and vibration and was replaced by the more familiar 6 cylinder, 3.4 litre XK unit that propelled the XK120 to its eponymous 193 kmph (120 mph).

Sir Stirling Moss (1929–)

Undoubtedly one of the most talented racing drivers ever to get behind the wheel, Sir Stirling Moss competed in almost every kind of motorsports event during a professional career in which he entered almost 600 races, winning 212 of them. He has raced an amazing 80 different types of car including the Mercedes-Benz 300 SLR in which he won the Mille Miglia and Targa Florio in 1955. Moss saw the transition from front-engined cars to rear- or mid-engined machines in Formula 1, racing the Mercedes-Benz W196 (in which he won the 1955 British Grand Prix at Aintree) as well as Cooper Climax and Lotus cars. He drove for Jaguar and Mercedes at Le Mans and won 16 Grand Prix races over a six-year period to become runner-up in the Formula 1 Drivers' Championship four times before his career was cut short by a near-fatal accident racing a Lotus 18 at Goodwood in 1962.

MERCEDES·BENZ

tilkæmper sig i hård kamp mod international konkurrence en overlegen dobbelsejr i

GRAND PRIX AF FRANKRIG 1954

1. Juan Manuel Fangio
2. Karl Kling

Sejrer Mercedes-Benz, dog vinderen af Donna Ci... i en Mercedes-Benz-vogn, i hvilket alle væddeløbserfaringer bliver ...

Printed in Germany (dan.)

Mercedes-Benz Type W196 R Poster

The Austrian artist Hans Liska, born in Vienna in 1907, actually trained as an accountant before deciding that he could make a living from his talent as a painter and illustrator. He became one of the most famous Second World War Axis artists, painting and sketching German combatants, their aircraft and armoured vehicles, in detailed and emotive battle scenes as part of the Nazi propaganda drive. After the war, Liska worked for magazines and in advertising, with Mercedes-Benz as one of his clients. This enthralling image of Karl Kling's Mercedes-Benz type W196 R, with its streamlined bodywork, thundering to second place in the 1954 French Grand Prix at Reims is one of many poster artworks produced by Liska for Mercedes. Fangio took first place in his W196 (his bore the number 18) and their Mercedes team-mate Hans Hermann set the fastest lap, all in the debut race for the new German Silver Arrow.

CIRCUIT ROUEN les ESSARTS - 7 JUILLET 1957
ASSOCIATION SPORTIVE DE L'A.C. NORMAND

Geo Ham

43e GRAND PRIX DE L'A. C. F.

Programme officiel : 100 fr.

STATION SERVICE
PHILIPS
AUTORADIO

PHILIPS

F. DUTERTRE
100, RUE LAFAYETTE
ROUEN - Tél. 71. 74-41

ENGAGÉS DU 43e GRAND PRIX DE L'A.C.F.
(SUITE)

12 Peter COLLINS (3rd)
FERRARI
+ 20 mins. behind
secs

14 Mike HAWTHORN (4th)
FERRARI
1 lap behind

16 M. TRINTIGNANT
FERRARI
Retired on Lap 24
Ignition Trouble

18 Stirling MOSS S. LEWIS-EVANS
VANWALL
Retired on Lap 31,
steering and overheating

20 Roy SALVADORI
VANWALL
Retired on lap 26 with
broken valve-spring

22 M. MacDOWELL (7th)
COOPER
9 laps behind (shared with Jack Brabham)

CARROSSERIE
DUBUC
RUE FRANÇOIS-ARAGO-ROUEN
— TÉLÉPHONE : 71. 59-33 —
REDRESSAGE DE CARROSSERIE
SUR MARBRE DE CONTROLE
(SEULE GARANTIE DE SÉCURITÉ)

Transports
Ténart
DÉMÉNAGEMENTS
TOUTES DESTINATIONS
▲
GARDE-MEUBLES
A CASES SÉPARÉES
▲
52, Rue de Lyons—ROUEN
Tél. 71 70.29   (Seine-Maritime)

1957 French Grand Prix Official Programme

The legendary Juan Manuel Fangio had raced for the Maserati team in 1954 for part of the season until Mercedes was ready to launch their W196 on the Grand Prix circuits and in 1957 he was back with the Italian team. Mercedes had withdrawn from racing after the Le Mans disaster in 1955 when one of their cars crashed into the crowd, killing the driver and more than 80 spectators. Fangio then drove for Ferrari in 1956, although he did not get on well with Enzo Ferrari and in 1957 he was back with Maserati, driving the same car – the 250F – that had helped him to become World Champion in 1954. The newly extended 6.5 kilometre (4 mile) circuit (it had previously been a little over 5 kilometres (3 miles) on public roads around the town of Les Essarts, about 12 kilometres (7.5 miles) south of Rouen, was the scene of Fangio's third Grand Prix victory of 1957. He had already won the Argentine and Monaco Grand Prix and taking the chequered flag in Rouen in July meant that his win at the Nurburgring a month later, made him World Champion for the fourth successive year.

Another legendary driver who made a name for himself with Ferrari was Englishman Mike Hawthorn (1929–1959). Hawthorn began his Formula 1 campaign with Cooper in 1952, taking fifth place in the World Drivers' Championship. Recruited to Ferrari the following season, Hawthorn also drove for Vanwall and Maserati in Formula 1 but it was with Ferarri that he won his world title in 1958. Hawthorn retired immediately afterwards and was tragically killed in a road accident in England the following year.

The final Formula 1 Champion of the 1950s was Jack Brabham (1926–2014), an Australian who had raced for Cooper, having helped to design their mid-engined cars which raced in Formula 1 and at the Indianapolis 500. Brabham would go on to take the World Championship title in 1960 and 1966, establishing his own racing team and becoming the only man ever to win the World Championship driving a car bearing his own name – the Brabham BT19.

It was during the 1950s that Formula 1 Grand Prix racing cars became recognizably different from sports racing cars. They became single-seat racers and, gradually, began to adopt a rear- or mid-engined layout. Sports racing cars,

LES CARS JOFFET

Services réguliers Voyageurs Messageries

Location de cars de 20 à 55 places
— pour excursions et Cérémonies —

GARE ROUTIÈRE - ROUEN
TÉL. 71. 40-26

ANSSELIN & Cⁱᴱ
TOUS LES PNEUS
RÉPARATIONS ★ RECHAPAGES
L'établissement le plus vaste et le plus moderne

STATION D'ÉQUILIBRAGE DE ROUEN - STATIQUE & DYNAMIQUE

51, RUE SAINT-JULIEN - **ROUEN** - TÉL. : 71. 45-01 (Derrière église Saint-Sever)

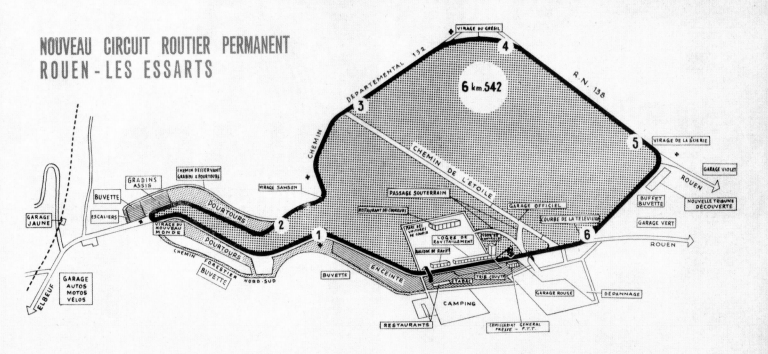

NOUVEAU CIRCUIT ROUTIER PERMANENT
ROUEN - LES ESSARTS

Buvez sur ce CIRCUIT
LA MANCHE Export *"Pils"*

Buvez sur ce CIRCUIT
Orange **FRESH** Citron

on the other hand, still looked much like the road-going machines on which they were often based, although these cars were also evolving into thoroughbred racers, as Jaguar ably demonstrated at Le Mans.

Jaguar had backed a team of three XK120 sports cars at Le Mans in 1950, learning from the experience to create the XK120 C (for "competition") to run in the 1951 race. The new "C-type" had bodywork that was more streamlined than the road car and used a more powerful version of the road car's 3.4-litre, six-cylinder engine. The C-type won the 1951 race ahead of a 4.5-litre Talbot-Lago and a 2.6-litre Aston Martin DB2. The following year, last-minute changes to the car to try to improve its aerodynamics caused overheating and all three Jaguars retired from the race, leaving the Mercedes-Benz 300 SL to take the trophy. In 1953, however, the C-type was back, taking first, second and fourth places. Jaguar's innovative use of disc brakes, seen on most modern cars today, on all four wheels made sure that the C-type had the stopping power to match its average speed of 170.34 kmph (105.85 mph) – the first time Le Mans had been won at an average above 160 kmph (100 mph).

Racing drivers could buy their own C-types to race at sports car events for a very reasonable (compared to other racing cars) US$6,000, which was roughly twice the price of a road-going XK120. By 1954, the C-type was becoming less competitive, although a privately entered car did finish fourth, and Jaguar was concentrating on its new racer, the D-type, which finished second behind Ferrari. The following year, the D-type was to dominate, Mike Hawthorn's Jaguar battling with Fangio's Mercedes 300 SLR until the German team retired after a tragic accident involving one of their cars. It is estimated that between 80 and 120 spectators were killed and scores more injured when the Mercedes crashed into the crowd.

In 1956 the D-type took first, fourth and sixth places at Le Mans and in 1957 first, second, third, fourth and sixth. Jaguar designer Malcolm Sayer (1916–1970), who created the C-type, D-type and the sensational E-type road car, had promised the Jaguar drivers that the D-type would do over 306 kmph (190 mph). It was timed on the Mulsanne Straight at 311 kmph (193 mph).

The Swinging Sixties

As the Sixties swung into fashion, it seemed that the car had attained its social status at every level that could be expected. It was a status symbol for those who felt the need to be overtly ostentatious; it was a necessity for those in rural areas who needed reliable transport; it was a mobile office for sales executives; it was an essential tool for the emergency services and the police, just as it was for the criminal fraternity; and yet the car could still be re-invented or redefined for new markets. The car still had a long way to go.

BELOW Paddy Hopkirk on his way to victory in the Mini Cooper S at the Monte Carlo Rally in 1964.

OPPOSITE The E-Type Jaguar offered stunning performance and breathtaking looks at a price that was only half that of other exotic sports cars. Like the humble Mini, the cool cat became a symbol of Sixties chic.

The 1960s saw the car take on the form of the humble Mini (see also page 79) – launched in 1959 but forever an icon of the Sixties – a car designed for frugality but adopted by the rich and famous as a symbol of Sixties "cool". Some sceptical motoring journalists who were invited to test drive the first Minis didn't actually believe that the little box with power to the front wheels would actually be able to go round corners. How wrong they were. The Mini became an instant hit as a saloon car

racer and as a rally car. It won the Monte Carlo Rally in 1964 and 1965 and would have won in 1966 but for some minor regulations which were thought to have been infringed. In any case, it won in Monte Carlo again in 1967.

The Mini began to appear in a number of different guises, with larger engines or different bodywork, but it was never intended to be a sports car. For those whose aspirations and bank balance could stretch to the purchase of an out-and-out sports car, there was ample choice of new models.

At the Geneva Motor Show in 1961, Jaguar launched the E-type. It was available as a soft-top or as a coupé with a neat, side-opening "hatch-back" and the 3.8-litre engine, although not race-tuned, was essentially the same as that used in the later Le Mans D-types. It could accelerate to 97 kmph (60 mph) from rest in a little over seven seconds and reach a top speed of around 240 kmph (150 mph). At a little over £2,000 in the UK and around $5,600 in America, the new Jaguar was barely half the price of, for example, Aston Martin's DB4. More than 50 years after it first appeared, the E-type is still in great demand and Jaguar designer Malcolm Sayer's exquisitely proportioned bodywork (see page 87) ensures that it continues to be commended by motoring enthusiasts and design experts as one of the most beautiful cars ever made.

Porsche announced a long-awaited replacement for their 356 in 1963 when the 911 was unveiled at the Frankfurt Motor Show. The 911 had a flat-six, air-cooled, boxer engine of 2 litres that gave the 911 its distinctive sound – like a Beetle that meant business – and it had the kind of performance that would be perfectly respectable from a fast car today. Acceleration to 97 kmph (60 mph) came in 8.3 seconds and the car charged on up to 209 kmph (130 mph). Porsche 911

derivatives would become faster and more sophisticated as the years progressed, the car staying in production in various forms until the present day.

The 911 looked unconventional compared to the E-type and was also more expensive at £2,996, while carrying a hefty price tag of $6,500 in America. If the 911 looked odd, then an even stranger car appeared in 1964 when the Lamborghini 350 GT came into being. Having driven some of the finest GT cars the established car makers had to offer, agricultural equipment manufacturer Ferruccio Lamborghini (see box feature page 95) decided that he could do better. He wanted a refined road car that was fast, quiet and comfortable. The V-12 engine that eventually powered his 350 GT certainly gave him the performance he craved and the car was engineered for superlative handling, but not everyone agreed that it looked the part. Only 120 would be built during its two-year production run and it is believed that the first of the 350 GTs were actually sold at a loss in order to keep the price competitive with the contemporary Ferrari, a 1964 275 GTB costing around £6,000, equivalent to more than US$17,000. Future Lamborghini cars would remain expensive, exclusive, and always bold in their styling.

OPPOSITE The Porsche 911 was launched in 1963 with a rear-engined layout and a distinctive shape that would persist for the next 50 years.

BELOW Lamborghini would earn a reputation for bold styling but the very first car, the 350 GT, had an awkward front end that was not to everyone's taste. Only 120 cars were made between 1964 and 1966.

The Japanese were also keen to experiment with sports cars, Datsun launching the first of its "Z Cars" – the 240 Z – in 1969 and Toyota producing its 2000 GT in 1967, although only 351 were ever made. There was no such limited production run for another famous Toyota name introduced in 1966, the Corolla. Subsequent Corolla models would keep the name alive for the next 50 years, with Corollas in production at manufacturing plants across the world from China to the UK and sales in excess of 35 million making it the world's best-selling car.

Another Japanese manufacturer, Honda, began to establish itself as a car manufacturer, rather than a motorbike company, with the N600, a Mini challenger that began to become available in Europe in 1968 and was launched in the US in 1969. It wasn't the only small car to try to claim some of the Mini's market share. Hillman had launched the Imp, a rear-engined car in the Mini class, in 1963, although it was dogged by development problems and industrial unrest. Hillman had been part of the British Rootes Group since 1931, but from the mid-1960s the Rootes Group was gradually bought out by Chrysler.

The idea of smaller cars began to catch on in America in the Sixties, but the American idea of a small car didn't really correspond to the European model. All of the major manufacturers tried their hand with "compact" cars and Chrysler's was the Valiant, subsequently marketed under the Plymouth brand. The same company, therefore, was selling a small car in Europe, the Hillman Imp, which was under 3.7

m (12 ft) long, while also selling a "compact" car in America, the Valiant, which was well over 4.6 m (15 ft) long. The truth was that Americans didn't really want small cars at that time. They wanted roomy cars with big V-8 engines, and with "gas" costing only 30 cents a gallon, fuel economy wasn't really a concern.

While saving fuel may not have been the biggest talking point in the 1960s, safety was becoming an issue. In Britain, and across Europe, new motorways were being built that were said to be designed for speeds up to 160 kmph (100 mph), and many countries, including Britain, had no speed restrictions on their motorways. Horrendous multi-car accidents in poor visibility led to Britain introducing the 70 mph (approximately 110 kmph) speed limit in 1965. Car manufacturers were certainly taking safety seriously. Flashing indicator lights were now standard on most cars, as were electric windscreen wipers and heaters that "demisted" the windscreen for clearer visibility. Volvo began to set the pace as far as safety features were concerned when the 144 went into production in 1966. The car had a fail-safe double braking system with highly efficient disc brakes on all four wheels, crumple zones front and rear to protect the passenger cabin, an interior designed to be devoid of protrusions to increase passenger safety in the event of an accident, and seatbelts fitted as standard for the driver and front-seat passenger. Volvo's reputation for safety was to become a major selling point for the company.

PREVIOUS PAGES Porsche's first sports car, the 356, had been extremely successful. However, the 911 (pictured), introduced in 1963 would go on to eclipse even its predecessor, becoming possibly the most popular sports car ever.

OPPOSITE The 1969 Datsun 240 Z had the look of a European sports car, although it was designed in Japan, and had the performance to match its looks. It became bigger and bulkier as it progressed through its 260 Z and 280 Z incarnations, losing much of its earlier appeal.

BELOW Big and bulky were positive assets for Volvo's 144 when it became the safest car on the road in 1966, establishing Volvo's enviable reputation for passenger protection.

Ferruccio Lamborghini (1916–1993)

Having been born into a family whose main interest was growing grape vines, it was almost inevitable that the mechanically minded Ferruccio Lamborghini would turn his talents to the manufacture of tractors and agricultural equipment. He maintained military vehicles while serving with the Italian Air Force during the Second World War, and was soon building tractors using military surplus. By 1959, Lamborghini was moving into the heating and air-conditioning business; he became a wealthy man, indulging himself with the best luxury sports cars available before deciding that he could build better and becoming a car manufacturer. The "Raging Bull" emblem that he adopted reflected Ferrucio's love of bullfighting and one of his most famous cars, the Miura (see pages 105, 116), was named after his friend Don Eduardo Miura (dates unknown) who bred fighting bulls on his ranch in Seville in Spain.

Muscle Cars

A street-scorching phenomenon burst into life in the American car market in the 1960s when the major manufacturers vied with each other to produce the fastest, most powerful, most awesome versions of their standard offerings, to be dubbed "muscle cars".

The muscle car had its roots in the hot-rod craze that had begun in the 1930s. Hot rods (the term is a short form of "hot roadster") were ordinary production models, like the Model T, that were stripped of luxuries to save weight; had their coachwork altered, with the engine panels or the roof removed; had the entire body adapted to sit lower on the chassis; and, crucially, were fitted with bigger, more powerful engines. The cars were pitted against each other in straight-line races either in the street (the main street of a small town was often referred to as the "main drag" which is where the term "drag race" originates), in flat desert space or on a disused airfield. Many of the young men returning from military service in the Second World War in 1945 had been trained as mechanics and they were keen to put their skills to work creating hot rods to compete in drag races.

Manufacturers quickly recognized the demand for more power, producing cars like the 1949 Oldsmobile Rocket 88, fitted with a newly developed 5-litre, V-8 engine. The Oldsmobile made its mark on the nascent NASCAR (National Association for Stock Car Auto Racing) events, becoming a force to be reckoned with as the car was further developed over the next three years. One of the Rocket's

greatest NASCAR rivals was the Hudson Hornet, introduced in 1951 with a 5-litre, six-cylinder engine which, when tuned for racing, was claimed to take the car to 180 kmph (112 mph).

In 1955, Chrysler produced the C-300 with a 5.4-litre V-8 engine that would take the car to almost 209 kmph (130 mph). The car was designed to use body parts from other Chryslers, but achieved a distinctive, purposeful style nevertheless, helping to define the new breed of muscle cars. A typical muscle car was a two-door coupé with seats for four adults. It needed to have rear-wheel drive with power from as big a V-8 up front as could be shoe-horned under the bonnet. It had to be able to give a good account of itself whether screeching away from traffic lights or thundering along a traditional 0.4-km (quarter-mile) drag strip, and it had to come at an affordable price.

ABOVE The Chevrolet Camaro appeared in 1966 as a counter to Ford's Mustang and was one of a breed known as "pony cars". These cars were sports coupés rather than souped-up sedans but the differences between a pony car and a muscle car are often quite vague.

ABOVE A 1971 Pontiac Firebird Trans Am prepares to put its 7.5-litre powerplant to the test on a drag strip. The car could reach 100 kmph (60 mph) from a standing start in around 7 seconds.

OVERLEAF The 1969 Dodge Charger Daytona proving that it is not, in fact, as long as a train. The heavily modified car with its streamlined nose cone and 60-cm- (two-foot-) high wing on the rear deck was designed to win NASCAR races, which it duly did, with only 503 examples made.

Muscle cars began to achieve supercar performance figures in the 1960s with Pontiac producing the trend-setting GTO in 1964. General Motors had withdrawn from racing official, factory-sponsored cars, which came as a real blow to the marketing men whose job it was to reach the younger clientele – the age group most influenced by speed and power. One group of Pontiac executives, led by Pontiac's charismatic chief engineer John DeLorean (see box feature), decided to take the two-door version of their new, basic Tempest saloon and fit a 6.4-litre V-8 that produced 325 bhp (brake horse power – the universal method of measuring an engine's power output). An average saloon car today produces less than half that amount of power. It was enough to give the new Tempest a 0–100 kmph (0–60 mph) acceleration time of less than seven seconds. There was soon an enlarged, race-tuned version of the engine that would reduce that time to just 4.6 seconds. DeLorean designated the new model GTO after the Ferrari 250 GTO, the GTO in the Ferrari title standing for Gran Turismo Omologato. For the Ferrari, this meant that it was a GT car of which enough had been built for sale to the public for it to qualify (or be homologated) to race as a production GT car. For the Pontiac GTO, it simply meant that it was borrowing some Ferrari gloss to highlight its own impressive performance.

Other muscle cars existed in small numbers, with Ford having produced a lightweight version of the Galaxy in limited numbers in 1963 as well as the Thunderbolt, a "muscled" version of their Fairlane saloon. The GTO, however, was intended for volume production, GM estimating that they would sell 5,000 in the first year. They had orders for 10,000 before the production line started to roll

John DeLorean (1925–2005)

One of the most colourful characters to emerge from the US car industry in the 1960s, an industry that has never known a lack of extrovert personalities, was John Zachary DeLorean. Born in Detroit, DeLorean was the eldest son of a Romanian immigrant father and Austrian mother. He studied industrial engineering at the Lawrence Institute of Technology and served with the US Army during the Second World War. He worked for Chrysler while completing his studies, then moved to Packard before joining the engineering staff at Pontiac. DeLorean was one of those responsible for the Pontiac GTO muscle car and the Pontiac Firebird. He became head of Pontiac in 1965 and was put in charge of GM's Chevrolet division in 1969. Leaving GM in 1973, he formed the DeLorean Motor Company with a manufacturing plant in Belfast, Northern Ireland. The company's only product, the DMC-12, was designed by Giugiaro (see box feature page 116), Renault-powered and engineered by Lotus. Financial irregularities and DeLorean's involvement in a planned drugs-smuggling enterprise to prop up the ailing company led to his downfall and the factory's closure in 1982. DeLorean ended his days in New Jersey, running a business selling designer wristwatches.

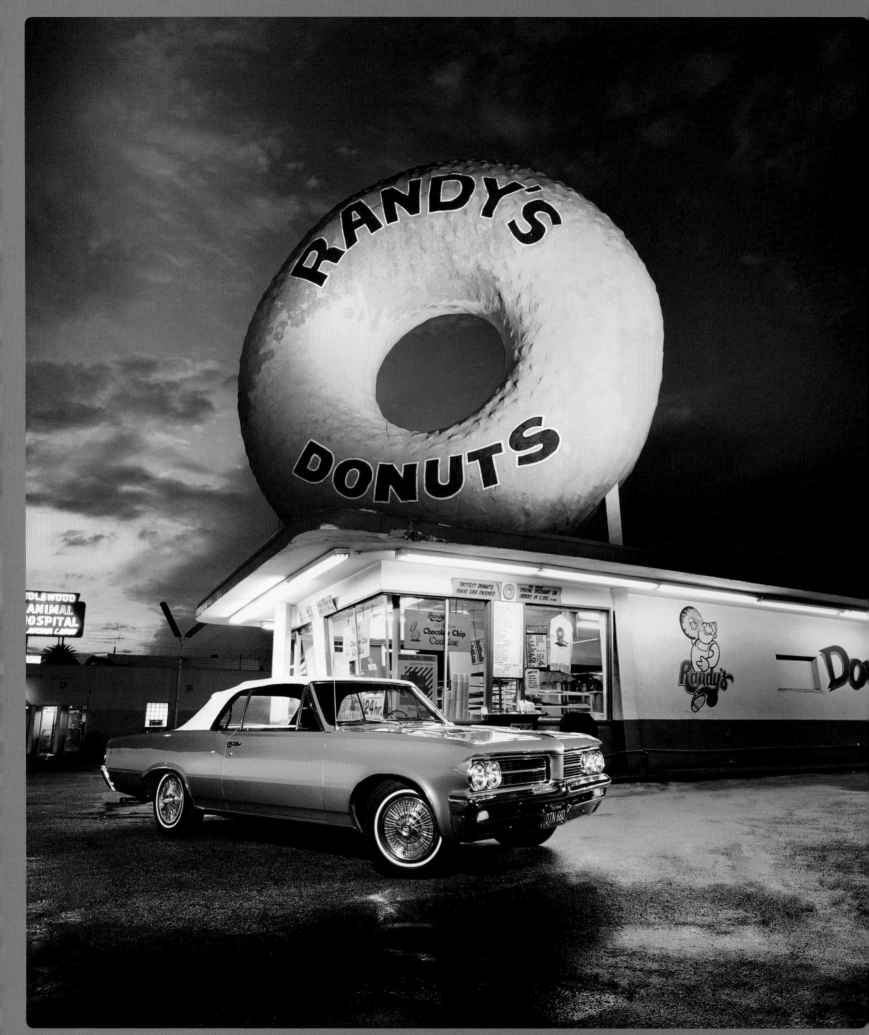

and went on to sell over 30,000 in 1964. The same was true of Plymouth's Road Runner. Chrysler expected to sell around 2,000 of the Plymouth muscle car when it was launched in 1968 – they sold 45,000.

Another type of muscle car began to appear when, instead of simply using one of their existing saloons as the basis for a sporting performance model, Ford decided to design a new sports coupé from scratch. Ultimately, the car actually used stock parts from a variety of other Ford models, including the Falcon, but the car that reached the marketplace in 1964 had a style of its own and the name, Mustang, that inspired a whole new range of "pony cars". Ford's new "2+2", a two-seater with two rear seats for occasional use, was stylish but lacked the power of the big muscle cars.

That power would be added with bigger engines as time went on. It certainly did not hamper sales. Ford expected to sell less than 100,000 Mustangs in the first year but were to sell 10 times that number over the first 18 months of the car's life. With such success comes competition. The Plymouth Barracuda actually made it to the marketplace a fortnight before the Mustang in April 1964 and they were to be joined over the next couple of years by a host of others, including the Chevrolet Camaro and its sister car, the Pontiac Firebird. The difference between the pony cars and the muscle car range was really that the pony cars looked more like sports cars while the ever-expanding range of muscle cars, which by 1966 included the famous Dodge Charger, looked more like beefed-up, two-door versions of standard saloons.

Muscle cars were incredibly fast in a straight line, faster than many of the quickest European sports cars of the day, but they were deliberately brutal machines with their roots in street drag racing, and did not handle, corner or brake as well as traditional sports cars. The muscle-car makers did, however, achieve their goal of making the cars affordable, with a Road Runner priced at under US$3,000 and a Pontiac GTO, loaded with all of the expensive factory options, coming in at around US$4,500. A Ferrari 250 GTO cost US$18,000 and buyers had to be personally approved by Enzo Ferrari himself!

ABOVE Steve McQueen as Lieutenant Frank Bullitt used his 1968 Ford Mustang fastback to pursue the bad guys (in a 1968 Dodge Charger) through the streets of San Francisco in one of cinema's greatest car chases in the movie.

OPPOSITE The car that started the 1960s muscle car craze was the 1964 Pontiac GTO, which unashamedly kidnapped its name from Ferrari.

OVERLEAF The new Ford Mustang, which was introduced to the public on April 17, 1964 at the New York World's Fair, Florida, 1963.

The Car's the Star

Nothing is more glamorous than being seen in a glitzy automobile, except perhaps being seen in a glitzy Hollywood movie. The motor industry and the movie industry have grown up together, with the first public screenings of very basic moving images taking place around 1895, only a few years after the first petrol-powered cars started to appear on the roads.

As movies became more sophisticated, with cinemas drawing huge audiences, the motor car began to stake its place as a movie star. No film was complete without some kind of car stunt, whether it was the Keystone Cops dangling off the outside of their police car or Laurel and Hardy smashing, crashing, crushing and even sawing in half the Model T Fords that made regular guest appearances in their films. There were some cars, however, that demanded more than just "bit-parts" – they had the presence to become real stars.

Probably the most famous of the star cars is James Bond's Aston Martin DB5. First seen in *Goldfinger* (1964), Q's (see box feature page 105) masterpiece was equipped with machine guns behind the sidelights, a bullet-proof rear screen, a radar tracking device, tyre slashers in the wheel hubs, revolving number plates, the ability to spray water or oil at the rear and, of course, the passenger ejector

ABOVE Sean Connery as agent 007 with his Aston Martin DB5 on a Swiss mountain road contemplating how to foil the evil Auric Goldfinger, from the movie of the same name.

ABOVE Bond's latest incarnation, Daniel Craig, with the Aston Martin DBS used in the 2006 movie *Casino Royale*.

RIGHT (BOX) The most famous "Q" was Desmond Llewelyn, who played the character in 17 Bond movies starting with *From Russia With Love* in 1963 and making his final appearance in *The World Is Not Enough* in 1999. He died in a car accident in 1999 at the age of 85. The role was later played by John Cleese.

seat. Bond flirted with a variety of sporty types, including a Sunbeam Alpine in the first movie, *Dr. No* (1962); BMW's Z3 in *Goldeneye* (1995) and Z8 in *The World Is Not Enough* (1999); the Lotus Esprit that could turn into a submarine in *The Spy Who Loved Me* (1977) and *For Your Eyes Only* (1981); and had dalliances with scores of models, but his heart remained true to Aston Martin. The DB5 returned in *Thunderball* (1965) and enjoyed cameo appearances in *Goldeneye*, *Tomorrow Never Dies* (1997) and *Casino Royale* (2006), although the 30-year-old car would have stood no chance racing Xenia Onatopp's brand new Ferrari F355 GTS in the hills above Monte Carlo in *Goldeneye*... unless Q had been doing some major tinkering. Aston Martins were also the superspy's supercars when he used a DBS in *On Her Majesty's Secret Service* (1969), a V8 Vantage in *The Living Daylights* (1987), a V12 Vanquish in *Die Another Day* (2002) and a DBS V12 in *Casino Royale* and *Quantum of Solace* (2008).

Another Aston Martin, this time a DB4 convertible, was driven by Michael Caine as Charlie Croker in *The Italian Job*. The real stars of the film were the Minis that led the Italian police Alfa Romeo Giulias a merry dance around Turin, but the film also featured a couple of E-type Jaguars that were smashed up by a mafia bulldozer (later restored in real life) and a Lamborghini Miura (see page 95) that was destroyed at the beginning of the film. In fact, the Miura was unscathed and the car that was seen being bulldozed over a cliff was a Miura wrecked in a real-life car crash. When the DB4 suffers the same fate, it is actually another vehicle "dressed" to look like the Aston Martin.

Major Geoffrey Boothroyd, "Q"

James Bond, the world's most famous spy, would be lost without his home-base back-up trinity of "M" (his boss), Miss Moneypenny (the boss's secretary) and Major Geoffrey Boothroyd, better known as "Q". The character received only fleeting mentions in most of Ian Fleming's original novels, the first of which was *Casino Royale* in 1953, and Fleming only deigned to give him a name when a firearms expert wrote to him pointing out that Bond was not always going into the field carrying the best available equipment. The expert's name was Geoffrey Boothroyd and Fleming named the character after him. "Q" (the designation stands for "Quartermaster") appeared in all but one of the official James Bond movies, supplying 007 with all manner of equipment including his Walther PPK handgun, an exploding briefcase, an exploding pen, an exploding cigarette pack and, of course, that gadget-laden Aston Martin DB5.

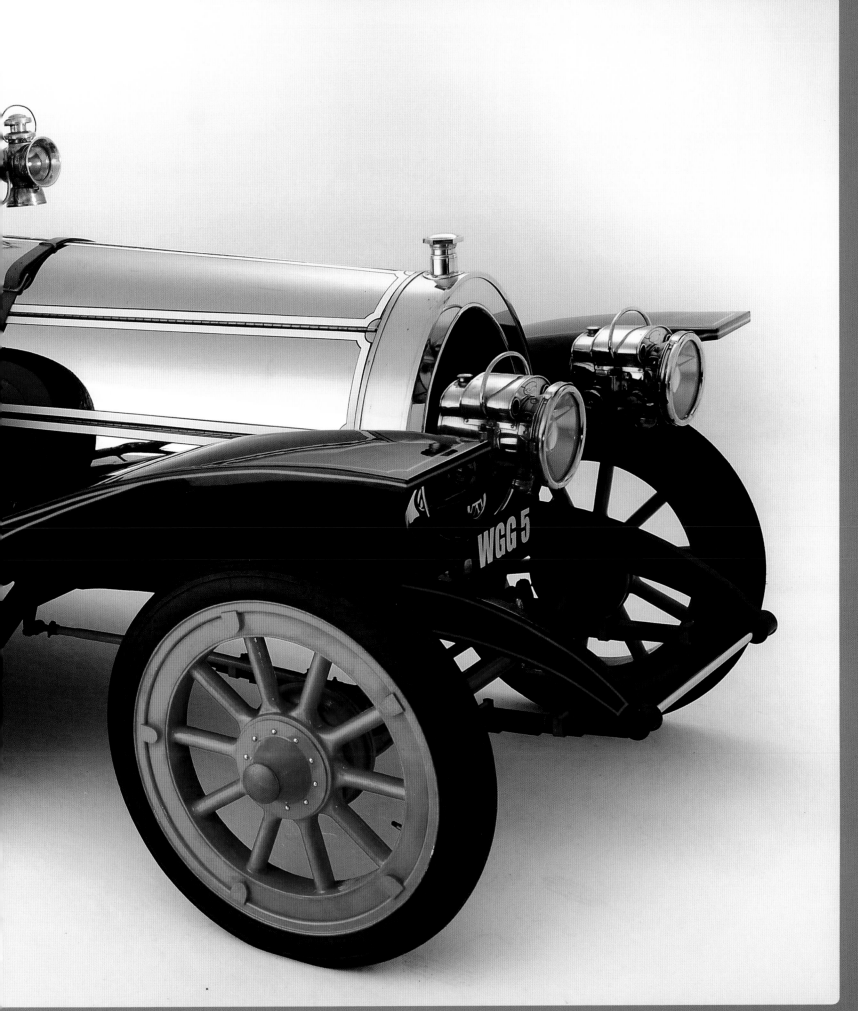

Just as Bond had no exclusive right to the Aston Martin, neither did Q have a monopoly on non-standard options. Doc Brown added a significant new feature to the DeLorean DMC-12 in *Back To The Future* (1985) – it could travel through time, and did so again in two sequels. There were few cars, however, that could swim, fly, think and even talk. The VW Beetle in the *Herbie* movies came close, but *Chitty Chitty Bang Bang* (1968) takes the prize. Six cars were actually built for filming, although only one was initially fitted with an engine, a 3-litre Ford V6, and fully equipped to drive on the road. Others were subsequently made roadworthy to publicize the film. The name Chitty Chitty Bang Bang actually came from a series of real cars with massive aero engines that raced at Brooklands in the 1920s, while the film was based on a children's novel by none other than Ian Fleming (see box feature page 105).

While it is perfectly normal for cars to talk to their drivers nowadays – sat-nav systems and audible warnings having been around for some time – holding a conversation with your vehicle only ever used to happen when it went wrong and needed to be shouted at. Not so for Michael Knight, whose Pontiac Trans Am, KITT (Knight Industries Two Thousand), chatted with great intelligence as they foiled the bad guys together in TV's *Knight Rider* (1982–1986). KITT could perform some amazing stunts, including turning himself into a Ford Mustang for subsequent movie and TV spin-offs, but for "daredevil, side-slippin', creek-jumpin', Dixie-tootin'" action, it was hard to beat the General Lee in *The Dukes of Hazzard* (1979). The show

ran for six years and almost 300 1968/69 Dodge Chargers were painted "flame red" orange with the Confederate flag on the roof and the racing number "01" on the doors. They needed so many because, on the big jumps, the crash landing invariably destroyed the car, no matter how it eventually appeared on screen.

TV crime fighters simply have to have a distinctive car to suit their characters. Starsky's custom-painted 1974 Ford Gran Torino suited his extrovert character in *Starsky & Hutch* (1975) while Triumph's TR7 was a neater solution for Purdey in *The New Avengers* (1976) but the most sedately driven TV-cop car was undoubtedly Morse's 1960 Mark 2 Jaguar in *Inspector Morse* (1987). The burgundy Jaguar was restored when it retired from showbusiness and sold for over £100,000 – superstar earnings for a 50-year-old car that originally cost under £1,500.

PREVIOUS PAGES The *Chitty Chitty Bang Bang* film car replica.

OPPOSITE ABOVE Minis ran riot through municipal buildings in Turin in the 1969 movie *The Italian Job* after the theft of a fortune in gold from Fiat.

OPPOSITE BELOW Dustin Hoffman drove an Alfa Romeo Spider in the 1967 movie *The Graduate*. Alfa Romeo produced a "Graduate" Spider model in time for the 20th anniversary of the movie.

BELOW In the *Inspector Morse* TV show, author Colin Dexter's character Morse, played by actor John Thaw, enjoyed the good things in life – classical music, real ale and his Mark II Jaguar.

The Motoring World in Crisis

Just when it seemed that the world's motor manufacturers had thought of every type of vehicle – from small city cars to exotic supercars – with which they could tempt the motorist, a new market began to take shape. Sporty types who like to go hunting, shooting, fishing, riding, skiing, hiking or otherwise take to the great outdoors were well served with the functional and rugged Jeep (see page 67) or Land Rover (see page 65), different versions of which had developed practical, estate-car-type derivatives. These four-wheel-drive cars performed well off-road, but lacked comfort, refinement and adequate cruising speed on the highway. What was needed was an off-road vehicle that could take its occupants from the driveway outside their homes, out onto the motorway in speed and comfort, then on into the fields and forests.

BELOW The idea for a larger, more luxurious version of the Land Rover dated back as far as 1951. The concept was abandoned in the late 1950s, only to re-emerge in the mid-Sixties and develop into the Range Rover. An early Range Rover was exhibited in the Louvre gallery in Paris as an outstanding example of modern sculpture.

The International Harvester Scout, built in Fort Wayne, Indiana, came along in 1961. Intended to compete directly with the Jeep CJ (Civilian Jeep), it was certainly every bit as basic as the Jeep. Later models would have more powerful engines, heaters and more comfortable seats, but the Scout models still lacked the sophistication of a road car. Nevertheless, the car attracted an enthusiastic following and stayed in production for almost 20 years. The Ford Bronco was Ford's first offering to this emerging market in 1966, improving the level of on-road performance but offering optional extras such as a snow plough and a post-hole digger still tended to give the car an agricultural feel. With the much larger Chevrolet Blazer, based on a shortened truck chassis with more cabin space, more power and greater comfort, expected in 1969, Rover's man in America needed something a cut above the current Land Rover offerings to help him compete. A Land Rover 88 was converted to take a Buick V-8 engine and sent to Solihull in England where Land Rover engineers took a long hard look. Rover had in fact been considering various ideas to expand the Land Rover range for a number of years and the 3.5-litre Buick V-8 made a lot of sense. The

aluminium engine block made it light enough to be used in Rover's executive saloon cars as well as in their 4 x 4 vehicles.

The new Range Rover was launched in 1970. It could carry five people in the sort of comfort and luxury that was expected in a Rover saloon (the British Prime Minister's official car was a Rover) at speeds on the road in excess of 160 kmph (100 mph), yet had permanent four-wheel drive, power-assisted disc brakes on all four wheels, corrosion-resistant aluminium bodywork and an off-road performance that was second to none. The era of the luxury SUV (Sports Utility Vehicle) had arrived.

Rover was not the only British company to adopt a V-engine around this time. Jaguar had developed its own 5.3-litre V-12 intended for its highly regarded XJ saloon. The car had been launched in September 1968 with Jaguar founder Sir William Lyons (see box feature page 62) describing it in television advertisements the following year as "the finest Jaguar ever" and the magazine *Autocar* hailing it as "the

smoothest and quietest car we have ever driven or been driven in…. Dynamically it has no equal at any price". With the new V-12 engine, as opposed to the old 4.2-litre, six-cylinder engine that had been in use since 1948, the 1972 XJ12 was the fastest four-door saloon car in the world, with a top speed of around 225 kmph (140 mph).

But did the world really need big engines and faster cars? The heady days of 1960s excess were fast disappearing in a smog of exhaust-fumed nostalgia as a recession began to bite in January 1973. The world's stock markets were then sent into freefall in October by an OAPEC (Organization of Arab Petroleum Exporting Countries) oil embargo imposed on Western countries in retaliation for the United States supporting Israel during the 1973 Arab–Israeli War. Oil prices soared, pay freezes led to industrial unrest and speed limits were imposed to try to conserve fuel.

In 1974, the US government declared a national 55 mph (about 90 kmph) speed limit. In Britain the limit, formerly 70 mph (about 110 kmph) on motorways, was reduced to 50 mph (80 kmph). The British motor industry reeled under a series of strikes, causing loss of production and quality-control problems that dealt it a blow from which it was never really to recover. Other British workers found themselves reduced to a three-day week to save power when coal miners went out on strike, and there were regular power cuts to homes across the country. By 1975 inflation in Britain was running at 25 per cent and most other industrial nations were suffering in a similar way.

Yet the oil crisis never really forced the fast car to become unfashionable. In 1978 the Chevrolet Corvette celebrated its 25th anniversary with a special two-tone, silver-over-black paint scheme. With a 5.7-litre engine, as opposed to the thirstier 7.4-litre version, the car could achieve around 4.5 km per litre (12 miles per gallon). It was later estimated that the 55 mph (90 kmph) speed limit, part of a fuel-saving package that had been intended to cut fuel consumption by 2.2 per cent, had actually saved less than half that amount each year. Crisis – what crisis?

ABOVE One of the cars that bucked the trend towards less thirsty engines was Jaguar's XJS in 1975, powered by a 5.3-litre V-12 engine.

BELOW The Giugiaro-designed Lotus Esprit was launched in 1976 and was to undergo continuous development while in production over the following 28 years.

Colin Chapman (1928–1982)

An engineer and designer of huge invention and influence, Colin Chapman began his motor-racing career driving modified Austin Sevens that he had adapted himself. He called his first car Lotus and, having spent two years in the RAF, continued to build and race a succession of Lotus specials. He established Lotus Cars as a company in 1952, at first running the company on a part-time basis with the help of volunteer enthusiasts. He was asked to design a new car for Vanwall in 1956 and it was with his car that Vanwall won the Constructors' World Championship in 1958. In the meantime, Lotus Cars had begun to take off with the Lotus Seven (still in production over 50 years later as the Caterham Seven). Lotus sports cars quickly gained a reputation for radical design, superior handling and high performance, an image that was enhanced by the new, mid-engined Lotus cars that began to make their mark in Formula 1 racing in the early 1960s. Chapman was one of those who pioneered the use of "wings" on Formula 1 cars and one of the first to experiment with "skirts" to produce ground-effect down force. He died of a heart attack in 1982 at the age of 54.

OPPOSITE 1969 Ford Bronco offered optional extras such as a snow plough and a post-hole digger which gave the car an agricultural feel.

America wasn't the only country producing fast sports models. In 1975 Jaguar began production of the XJS coupé as a replacement for the ageing E-type, equipped with the 5.3-litre V-12 engine. The 225 kmph (140 mph) XJS was joined in the same year by BMW's 6-series coupé, which was only fractionally slower and replaced the BMW 3.0CSL, a car that had become famous as the "Batmobile" in the European Touring Car Championship races. Lotus launched its Esprit at the Paris Motor Show in 1975, the car going into production in 1976 and in 1978 Mazda put the RX-7 into production.

The RX-7 is notable because of its Wankel rotary engine, invented by a German engineer named Felix Wankel (1902–1988). The engine does not have pistons pumping up and down to turn a shaft, but uses the idea of the "four-stroke" combustion cycle applied in a way that misses out the vertical (or horizontal in the case of a boxer engine) pumping in favour of a direct spinning motion. A triangular rotor linked directly to the drive shaft spins inside a shaped chamber with the intake, compression, combustion and exhaust phases occurring as the fuel is "trapped" or swept out of different areas of the chamber. The first Wankel-engined cars were NSU models produced in the 1960s, although Mazda developed the engine more successfully and still uses it today. The rotary engine gave the RX-7 a smooth power delivery and was small enough to mount well behind the front wheels, endowing the car with excellent handling characteristics, although the original version was not scorchingly fast and the engine (equivalent to 2.3 litres) struggled to return 7 km per litre (20 miles per gallon).

A more practical performance car appeared in 1975 when Volkswagen revealed the Golf (also known as the "Rabbit" and "Caribe") GTI. The Golf was the replacement for the VW Beetle which, by 1972, had sold in excess of 15 million and become the first car to beat the Model T Ford's production record. In 1973, more than 16 million Beetles had been built and its successor was on the way. The 1974 Golf was available with engines ranging from 1.1 to 1.8 litres, two doors or four, plus a hatchback. It had front-wheel drive, excellent road-holding and, in GTI form with a 1.6-litre, fuel-injected engine, it could accelerate from 0 to 100 kmph (60 mph) in under nine seconds. That was good enough to keep up with, for example, an RX-7, and the frugal Golf returned over 12 km per litre (35 miles per gallon). Volkswagen had started a new craze with its "hot hatch".

Evolution of the Supercar

Some would argue that supercars have been part of car culture since the beginning of the motoring age. There have, after all, always been cars that are faster, more expensive or more luxurious than the average runabout, but the 1960s saw the emergence of a new type of exotic thoroughbred that marked the genesis of the modern supercar.

Prior to the 1960s, the fastest roadgoing sports cars generally had a direct racing pedigree. Before the Second World War, roadgoing sports cars like Bentleys or Mercedeses were often indistinguishable from the racing versions. Owners would drive their cars to events and drive them home again afterwards, always providing that both car and owner survived. In 1948 Jaguar produced the world's fastest road car with the XK120, which spawned the Jaguar C-Type racer, which was developed into the D-Type, which in turn evolved into the E-type. While the E-type became an icon of the 1960s and should qualify for supercar status with its gorgeous styling and top speed in excess of 225

kmph (140 mph), there were other, more exotic machines on the drawing boards, cars that were phenomenally fast but not intended for the racetrack, supercars that would carry a price tag only the super-rich could afford.

ABOVE In 1987 the Ferrari F40 became the first true road car with the ability to exceed 200 mph (322 kmph), but others were soon to join the exclusive 200+ club.

OPPOSITE In the McLaren F1 the driver sat in the middle with a terrified passenger on either side watching the scenery whizz by at up to 386 kmph (240 mph).

Giorgetto Giugiaro (1938–)

Born in Garessio in northern Italy, Giugiaro studied fine art before working for Fiat in Turin. By the time he was 21 he was working with the styling house Bertone before moving to Ghia in 1966 and setting up his own Italdesign company in 1968. Giugiaro has designed some of the world's most famous sports cars including the Alfa Romeo Giulia Sprint GT, Lotus Esprit, DeLorean, Maserati Ghibli and BMW M1, as well as lesser models such as the Morris Marina makeover, the Morris Ital. In 1999 Giugiaro was voted Car Designer of the Century.

The Lamborghini Miura (see also box feature page 95, and page 105), still regarded as one of the most beautiful cars ever made, took the Geneva Motor show by storm when the first complete prototype was unveiled there in 1966. The Miura's mid-engined layout had really only been seen on the racetrack before and the 3.9-litre V-12 produced a top speed of over 270 kmph (170 mph). When the first cars went on sale at US$20,000, they were roughly three times the price of an E-Type.

For car lovers with the deepest pockets, the Miura was soon joined by a tempting array of alternatives such as the Maserati Ghibli in 1967. A more traditional, front-engined design, the Ghibli's 4.7-litre V-8 propelled it to 100 kmph (60 mph) from a standing start in just 6.4 seconds. Ferrari's V-12-engined Daytona of 1968 could better that with a 5.4-second 0–100 kmph (0–60 mph) time. While not created specifically to be raced, cars with such breathtaking performance inevitably were, although it was as roadgoing supercars that they set the benchmark for everything that followed.

In the 1970s, despite the looming oil crisis (see page 111), the fuel-thirsty supercars really came into their own. De Tomaso produced the Pantera in Italy in 1971 with a mid-mounted Ford engine at the rear and Maserati introduced the rakish Khamsin in 1972, but the most outrageous supercar of the Seventies was launched at the Geneva Motor Show in 1971 – the Lamborghini Countach. Its sharp, angular bodywork and scissor doors, hinged at the front to open upwards, became trademarks of a car that would remain in production until 1990.

A supercar landmark was reached in the 1980s when the Ferrari F40 became the first road-legal car to break the 322 kmph (200 mph) barrier. The F40's only real competitors in the performance stakes were the latest Countach and Porsche's rear-engined, four-wheel-drive 959, but there were new names waiting to join the supercar league such as Zender whose Fact 4 BiTurbo was a masterpiece of modern supercar styling.

RIGHT Named after a breed of fighting bull (which in turn was named after its Spanish breeder), the beautiful Miura is arguably the most elegant car ever to emerge from the Lamborghini factory and, like the Lamborghini "raging bull" emblem, it reflected company founder Ferrucio Lamborghini's love of bull fighting.

Jaguar E-Type Design Drawing

This drawing from Jaguar's archives of a Series 1 E-Type is marked with a range of internal cockpit dimensions but also shows the smooth lines and finely balanced proportions of the original E-Type design. Jaguar designer Malcolm Sayer famously spent hours with a slide rule and log tables calculating the exact trajectory of curves that would provide not only aerodynamic efficiency but also a sleek shape that was pleasing on the eye. From its launch in Geneva in 1961 the E-Type (known as the XKE in the United States) was hailed as one of the most beautiful cars ever made. Although its original lines were seriously compromised by the time the bloated V12 2+2 coupe appeared ten years later, the early E-type received countless plaudits, including being adopted as part of its permanent design collection by New York's Museum of Modern Art in 1996.

OPPOSITE Named after the French racing driver Pierre Veyron, who won the 24-hour Le Mans race in a Bugatti in 1939, the Bugatti Veyron was named *Top Gear* car of the decade in 2009. The Super Sport version is the fastest production car in the world, with a top speed of 431 kmph (268 mph).

BELOW RIGHT Often compared to the Ferrari Daytona, the sleek Maserati Ghibli was styled by Italian designer Giorgetto Giugiaro.

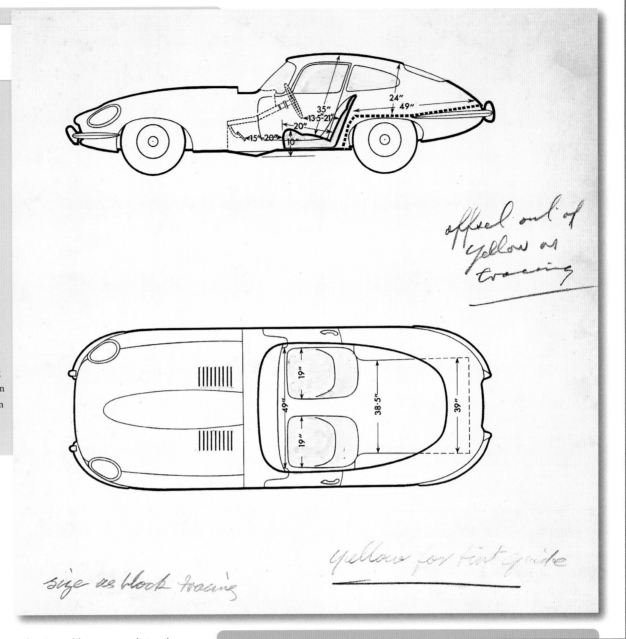

The supercars of the 1990s, however, were dominated by more traditional manufacturers. In 1992 Jaguar began production of the XJ220, a mid-engined 2-metre- (7-ft-) wide monster that could top 322 kmph (200 mph) but could not, in standard form, reach the 354 kmph (220 mph) suggested in its title. The Bugatti EB110 could keep up with the big Jag with a top speed of 343 kmph (213 mph), but the most sensational supercar of the 1990s was undoubtedly the McLaren F1. In the cockpit of the F1, the driver sat in the middle, flanked by two passenger seats, and could watch the speedometer climb to an amazing 386 kmph (240 mph).

The McLaren's crown as the world's fastest production car became the target for the twenty-first century supercars, now often referred to as hypercars, such as the Bugatti Veyron, the Pagani Zonda, the SSC Aero and the Koenigsegg. These cars use advanced electronics, lightweight carbon-fibre bodywork, computer-controlled engine management systems and good old-fashioned bhp to give them jet-aircraft acceleration times and top speeds over 402 kmph (250 mph). All of this comes at a price, of course, that keeps these most desirable of all supercars highly exclusive. If you're shopping for a hypercar, you'll need to have around US$2 million in your pocket.

Adolfo Orsi (1888–1972)

A successful industrialist who started out by building up his own scrap-metal business in the Modena area in northern Italy, Orsi went on to own steel mills. He bought Maserati when the three Maserati brothers who founded the company were suffering financial trouble in 1937. Orsi revitalized Maserati and when the different divisions of his corporation were split up in the 1950s, he retained the car company. He remained in control of Maserati well into the supercar era, finally selling his share of the business to Citroën in 1968.

The New Age Takes Shape

Ford had, by the 1980s, a somewhat undeserved reputation for conservative thinking when it came to car design. Like every other manufacturer, they had always been keen to appeal to the widest possible customer base and that meant keeping up with market trends, introducing new features when they were tried, tested and of proven reliability, and not frightening the Ford faithful with outlandish designs. There were, however, notable exceptions and the Ford Probe concept car unveiled in 1979 was one of them. This first probe was all sharp angles and glass, looking something like a shuttle craft from Star Trek's USS *Enterprise*, but by the time the Probe III came along in 1981, Ford's thinking had radically changed. The car had a smooth, aerodynamic shape with "spats" covering the rear wheels to reduce drag even further and a "biplane" twin rear spoiler.

Most concept cars are design exercises that never actually make it into production. Not so with the Probe III – it became the Ford Sierra. The Sierra's rounded shape earned it the nickname "the jelly mould" when this replacement for the box-like Cortina came along in 1982. Compared with modern cars, the shape doesn't really look very startling at all, but in the early 1980s, when Ford in America were still selling the cumbersome Fairmont, the new design was revolutionary. Sporting four doors, a hatchback, front-wheel drive and a striking resemblance to the Probe, it stopped short of adopting rear-wheel spats. Nor did it have a biplane rear spoiler, at least not at first. Since Volkswagen had invented the "hot hatch" with the Golf GTI in 1976, everyone else had produced their own high-performance versions of standard family hatchbacks. Peugeot introduced their 205 GTI in 1984 with a 1.6-litre engine, offering a 1.9-litre unit two years later that gave 130 bhp and a 0–97 kmph (0–60 mph) time of just 7.8 seconds. This

was a real challenger for the market-leading Golf, although Ford had also staked a claim in the hot-hatch gold rush with the Fiesta XR2 (1981), the larger Escort XR3 (1980) – both later available with fuel-injected engines as XR2i and XR3i – and the Sierra XR4i (1983). The three-door XR4i boasted the Probe III's biplane rear spoiler and a performance that could match the Peugeot 205 GTI.

Ford, of course, had produced high-performance sporting versions of its family saloon cars before. The Lotus Cortinas of 1963 and 1966 are obvious examples, reflecting Lotus's engineering expertise in producing high-performance cars. In 1979, Lotus had turned the mundane Chrysler Sunbeam into the Sunbeam Lotus, giving the little hatchback real presence on the road in a distinctive black-and-silver paint scheme. The 274 kmph (170 mph) Lotus Carlton, based on the Vauxhall Carlton saloon (Opel Omega in Europe), was a monster of a car with a turbocharged 3.6-litre engine that took it from 0 to 97 kmph (60 mph) in 5.2 seconds. For a road car in 1990 these were sensational figures, but for sheer sensationalism the Carlton could not compete with another Lotus-engineered car that predated it by almost 10 years.

In 1981 the first DeLorean DMC-12 rolled off the production line at a purpose-built factory in Dunmurry, just outside Belfast in Northern Ireland. The sleek sports car had gull-wing doors and bare-metal, brushed-stainless-steel bodywork. Designed by Giorgetti Giugiaro (see box feature page 116), it was the brainchild of former GM vice-president John DeLorean (see box feature page 97). The factory had been set up with the help of a £100 million grant from the British government, in an attempt to help alleviate the region's chronic unemployment problem. Just under two years and about 9,000 cars later, the venture collapsed under an avalanche of alleged financial irregularity, with John DeLorean battling accusations of drug trafficking.

DeLorean may have failed in Northern Ireland, but elsewhere business was booming as industry forged ahead in the wake of the recession-hit Seventies. The "yuppie" (young urban professional person) had emerged and, to make sure everyone recognized his or her success in business, chose to drive a German saloon car. BMW's new 3-series went into production in 1982 with a base price in America in excess of $18,000. It joined the new 5-series saloon, which was larger and more expensive, and the well-established, top-of-the-range 7-series. There were high-performance versions across the BMW range but there were also a number of diesel-engined options. BMW had not yet adopted an aero-dynamic, rounded style for its cars but hard lessons had been learned during the fuel crisis of the Seventies, petrol prices were higher than ever and diesel was growing in popularity. Streamlined styling could help to save petrol, but diesel fuel was cheaper at the pumps and diesel engines (which use the heat generated by compression to ignite

BELOW John DeLorean with his Belfast-built gull-wing DMC-12. Despite boasting engineering input from Lotus, the car was doomed to failure by financial problems and only 9,000 were produced. A starring role in the *Back To The Future* movie series, however, turned the car into a time-travelling legend.

Rudolf Diesel (1858–1913)

Born in Paris, to where his parents had migrated from Bavaria in Germany, Rudolf Diesel spent part of his childhood in Paris but was educated in Augsburg in Germany at a school where his uncle taught mathematics. He studied engineering in Munich and worked for a time in Switzerland before returning to Paris in 1880 to help design a refrigeration plant. Diesel experimented with engine design and almost died when one of his early efforts exploded. He persevered, however, developing a type of internal combustion engine that did not require a complicated electrical system to produce an ignition spark at the right time, instead using the heat created by the compression of the gas in the cylinder to ignite the fuel. Engines based on Diesel's design were robust, efficient and better in damp conditions than those relying on fragile electrics. This lead to their widespread use as marine engines. In 1913, Diesel disappeared overboard from the ship on which he was travelling to London for a business meeting, apparently having committed suicide.

BELOW Four-wheel-drive systems were heavy, expensive, slowed a car down and were only of use to farmers, country squires and squaddies – then in 1980, along came the Audi Quattro.

the fuel, rather than a spark) were gaining a reputation for being more reliable than petrol engines, with double the lifespan. Previously regarded as the sort of engine used only by farmers, the military, truckers and bus drivers, diesel engines were now widely available in cars from the most humble of small hatchbacks to the largest family saloons, although in America, where "gas" prices were kept low, diesel would take longer to catch on.

A yuppie, of course, was not really a diesel consumer. The yuppie needed to display an apparent disregard for frugality. With German engineering having established a reputation for high quality, at a high price, the yuppie might choose to drive the Porsche 944 in 1981, then trade that for a Porsche 911 Carrera in 1984, the latest incarnation of the 21-year-old 911. Priced at well over $30,000 in America, the 911 now had chunky bumpers, required on all vehicles for sale in the United States to comply with safety laws. The 911 was one of only a few sports cars that managed to incorporate the new bumpers without entirely ruining the overall design. Like most other performance cars, however, it was robbed of some of its power in complying with American emissions regulations. America, infamous for the big engines in its "gas-guzzler" cars, was leading the world in trying to curtail the motor car's output of environmentally harmful exhaust gases.

Another German company, Audi, part of the Volkswagen group following Volkswagen's takeover of the merged Auto Union and NSU companies (see page 54), launched the Quattro sports coupé in 1980, featuring permanent four-wheel drive, the first time such a system had been used on a sports car since the British Jensen FF in 1966. Because four-wheel drive offered good road-holding and performance no matter what the weather or road conditions, other manufacturers soon began to consider four-wheel drive for all sorts of road cars from the mighty Porsche 911 to the lowly Fiat Panda hatchback.

German manufacturers may have been enjoying a sales boom, but in Britain and America the outlook was far less optimistic. Nevertheless, America continued to develop the SUV (see page 111) trend with cars like the Jeep Cherokee (1984) and Dodge Raider (1987), although such cars were not always as American as they seemed. The Raider was actually a thinly disguised Mitsubishi Pajero. America could, however, lay claim to starting another trend in the 1980s when the Dodge Caravan minivan became the first MPV (Multi Purpose Vehicle) people carrier.

BELOW 1987 Porsche 911 3.2 Carrera.

Wild Beasts in the Wilderness

Rallying, like most motor sport, was once a competition between wealthy, enthusiastic amateurs. Major manufacturers often lent their support to the best of the amateur drivers in order that everyone would see how well their cars performed under arduous conditions, but the races were run and organized, in the main, by non-professional participants. That all began to change in the 1950s.

When motor sport began to rev its engine anew in the wake of the Second World War, the roads of Europe were once again opened for racing, albeit in a more controlled manner than in the past. Almost any car could be used, and was used, in rally racing. The large and graceful Jaguar Mk VII won the Monte Carlo rally in 1956 but around that time you would also have been able to see the Porsche 356, Volvo PV 444 saloon, Triumph TR3 sports car, Mercedes 300 SL or the

technically advanced Citroën DS competing in events with the cars running pretty much as standard road cars. Different types of car competed in different classes in rally races, but you were most likely to find the car's owner behind the wheel, enjoying the fun of driving fast in a spirited competition.

Manufacturers' teams, known as "works" teams, brought about huge changes in the way rallying was run. The public delighted in seeing cars that they could easily recognize as "normal" vehicles charging along mountain roads or sliding round corners

on forest tracks, but the works cars were seldom just standard vehicles with racing numbers stuck on the doors and bonnet. Proving that your car was tough and reliable enough to compete in a rally was one thing – showing that it was fast enough to win brought obvious benefits in terms of increased sales. Works rally cars were, therefore, fitted with more powerful engines, stripped of unnecessary trim and equipment to make them lighter and had improved suspension to help them handle better at speed. Rally cars still looked like the cars the general public saw in car showrooms or parked in the street, but under the skin they were evolving into something quite different.

The rules and regulations covering the different classes of rallying became ever more complex and detailed in order to keep up with the changes that the professional works teams wanted to make. The Mini (see chapters 14 and 16) made a huge impact on rallying with its front-wheel drive and nippy handling, winning the Monte Carlo Rally in 1963, 1964, 1965 and 1967. The works drivers also won in 1966, but were disqualified because they had the wrong kind of headlamp bulbs. The manufacturers had to take great care that their modifications did not contravene the regulations that were designed to try to stop anyone gaining an unfair advantage.

OPPOSITE The sensational Lancia Stratos goes boating during the World Rally Championship's Safari Rally in Kenya in 1976. With a Ferrari engine and Ferrari good looks, the Stratos was the glamour car of world rallying, even when fitted with bull bars.

ABOVE The Audi Quattro was to prove that four-wheel power outplayed two-wheel power in world rallying and other manufacturers were soon developing 4x4 systems for their own cars. Four-wheel drive only helped, of course, when the wheels were actually on the ground....

OVERLEAF The humble Mini Metro town car acquired four-wheel drive and a 3-litre, V-6 engine in the back where the shopping normally goes to compete as a Group B rally car between 1984 and 1986.

Tommi Mäkinen (1964–)

Four times World Rally Champion in 1996, 1997, 1998 and 1999, Tommi Mäkinen's hugely successful career in motor sport includes winning the Finnish National Ploughing Championship in 1982 and 1985. He is better known, of course, for driving slightly less agricultural machinery and has competed in the Lancia Delta Integrale, Ford Escort RS Cosworth, Ford Sierra RS Cosworth, Nissan Sunny, Mitsubishi Lancer Evo and Subaru Impreza, to name but a few. Born in Puupola in Finland, Mäkinen is one of the modern generation of "Flying Finn" rally drivers and is not related to the famous Timo Mäkinen (1938–), who won the 1965 Monte Carlo Rally in a Mini Cooper S – Mäkinen is the fourth-most-common name in Finland. Although Tommi Mäkinen retired from racing in 2003, he is still very much involved in the sport through his company, Tommi Mäkinen Racing, which runs a rally-driving school as well as supplying race-prepared cars, spare parts and technical support for rally teams.

By the mid-1960s the different classes of rally cars were organized into "Groups", just as they were in other forms of racing, and by the early 1970s, in order to ensure that manufacturers were actually building and offering for sale the cars that they were rallying, the Groups were designated as:

Group 1 – series production touring cars with 5,000 produced

Group 2 – touring cars with 1,000 produced

Group 3 – series production GT cars with 1,000 produced

Group 4 – special GT cars with 500 produced

Group 5 – sports cars with 25 produced

Group 6 – prototypes with no minimum production limit

The first car to be designed and purpose-built for rallying, with 496 produced to allow it to squeeze into Group 4, was the Lancia Stratos. With a mid-mounted V-6 engine from a Ferrari Dino powering the rear wheels, the road-going version of the car sprinted through 0–97 kmph (0–60 mph) in under 5 seconds. The Stratos won the World Rally Championship in 1974, 1975 and 1976. Although it relinquished its title to a more conventional saloon-type car, the Fiat 131 Abarth which won in 1977, 1978 and 1980, with the Ford Escort RS1800 winning in 1979, the Stratos showed what could be achieved with a truly specialized rally car.

The Stratos paved the way for the new "Group B" regulation cars in 1982. These were among the fastest pure rally cars ever built. Only 200 cars needed to be built for the vehicle to qualify and these included the Audi Quattro with a 2.1-litre turbocharged engine that provided 500 bhp and a 0–97 kmph (0–60 mph) sprint time of only 3 seconds. This was the first rally car successfully to employ four-wheel drive and, once the other manufacturers realized how effective a fast 4x4 sports car could be, an exciting new Group B breed emerged. Porsche's 911 became the 959 with four-wheel drive, Ford produced the mid-engined 4x4 RS 200, Lancia had their hugely successful Delta Integrale, and two "shopper specials" were given a bit of a makeover. The Peugeot 205 and the Mini Metro in normal guise were the kind of cars that your granny might use on her weekly run to the supermarket. But if she was to lift the hatchback on the 205 Turbo 16 or Metro 6R4 rally cars she would struggle to find somewhere to put the cat food and cereal. The cars, normally front-engined Roberto Giolito front-wheel drive, were transformed by mounting the engines behind the drivers, right where the shopping would normally go. The mild-mannered Mini Metro was given a 3-litre V-6 and both cars had four-wheel drive. Granny would never have got back from the shops so quickly.

The Group B cars were phenomenally fast, but this also led to a series of tragic accidents that ultimately saw Group B being abandoned. Other designated groups and classifications and an ever-growing list of regulations evolved over the years, but the Group B "wild beasts" laid the ground for the development of modern 4x4 rally cars such as the Ford Focus, the Citroën C4, the Subaru Impreza and the Mitsubishi Lancer Evo. Like their forebears, these cars bear only a passing resemblance to their road-going counterparts, but the engine can generally be found exactly where you would expect it!

ABOVE In the mid-1990s, the blue-and-yellow Subaru Imprezas driven by the likes of Colin McRae, Carlos Sainz and Richard Burns were the cars everyone had to beat and their success on the rally circuits turned the plain-looking road-going saloons into highly desirable performance cars.

BELOW A ninth-generation Mitsubishi Lancer Evo in the hands of Czech driver Martin Semerad, gliding sideways on the ice during the Swedish rally in February 2011

OPPOSITE Sebastian Loeb in his Citroën C4 WRC. He first drove the car in the Monte Carlo Rally in 2007, won the event and went on to win the championship, as he had done the previous year in a different Citroën and would do the following year. Up to 2011, Loeb had been World Champion a record seven times in succession.

Car Makers Go Global

Americans famously love their cars. By the middle of the 1980s, there were 137.3 million passenger vehicles on the road in the US – approximately one car for every 1.7 people, whether they were old enough to drive or not. In 1985, the nation's best-selling car was the North American version of the Ford Escort, the first front-wheel-drive car Ford had built in the United States. The second-best-seller was the Ford Taurus, reflecting some of the styling of the European Ford Sierra, and in third place was the Honda Accord.

Just a few years previously, the idea that a small car could be America's most popular would have been almost as unthinkable as the notion that a Japanese import could come third. Yet the Japanese imports had been sneaking in under the American public's radar for years. Chrysler had been selling the Dodge Colt since 1970, but it was actually a Mitsubishi Galant (and later the Mitsubishi Mirage) with a Dodge badge on the bonnet. The oil crisis of the 1970s that had sent fuel prices soaring, coupled with the stringent regulations concerning

safety and emissions that were being imposed by the American government, meant that the big, heavy, fuel-hungry highway cruisers America had produced in the past were going out of fashion faster than they could splutter to the gas station. The American public decided that they wanted cars that were cheaper to run and more reliable than domestic models. No less than 25 per cent of cars sold in America in 1980 were imports, an alarming figure when you consider that around 17 per cent of the American work force was involved in producing cars. Something had to be done.

Gustaf Larson (1887–1968)

Erik Gustaf Larson was a graduate in Mechanical Engineering from the Royal Institute of Technology in Stockholm, Sweden, and was a co-founder of the car maker Volvo in 1927 along with his friend Assar Gabrielsson (1891–1962). The first Volvo car, the ÖV4 , also known as the Jakob, was produced at a factory in Hisingen, Gothenburg in April 1927 and was specifically designed by Larson to be able to stand up to the harsh Swedish winters. Larson was vice president and technical manager of Volvo, working for the company up to his death in 1968. Under his guidance, Volvo achieved a name for safety, introducing the reinforced passenger safety cage and the first laminated windscreens in 1944, the first front-seat safety belts in 1959, front and rear crumple zones in 1966 and a host of other innovations on which the reputation of the company was built.

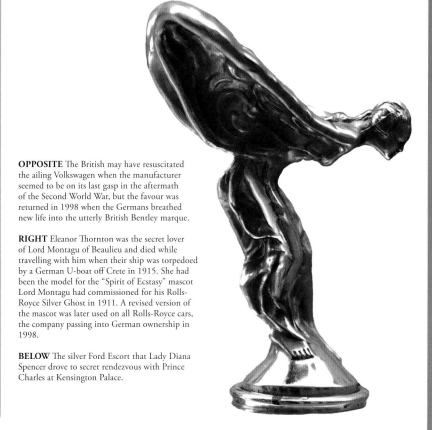

OPPOSITE The British may have resuscitated the ailing Volkswagen when the manufacturer seemed to be on its last gasp in the aftermath of the Second World War, but the favour was returned in 1998 when the Germans breathed new life into the utterly British Bentley marque.

RIGHT Eleanor Thornton was the secret lover of Lord Montagu of Beaulieu and died while travelling with him when their ship was torpedoed by a German U-boat off Crete in 1915. She had been the model for the "Spirit of Ecstasy" mascot Lord Montagu had commissioned for his Rolls-Royce Silver Ghost in 1911. A revised version of the mascot was later used on all Rolls-Royce cars, the company passing into German ownership in 1998.

BELOW The silver Ford Escort that Lady Diana Spencer drove to secret rendezvous with Prince Charles at Kensington Palace.

The solution came as a combination of government financial support, a reduction in the work force and a rationalization of the manufacturing process. In 1981 General Motors began producing its "J platform". The "platform" was basically a way of using the same components to manufacture a range of cars with different body styles to suit different market sectors. Sharing engines, gear boxes, electrical components, suspension and drive-train mechanicals as well as minor items right down to switches and door locks was the most economical way to produce a modern car. The J platform was utilized across the GM range from the Cadillac Cimarron and Oldsmobile Firenza to the Chevrolet Cavalier and Pontiac Sunbird. Around the same time, Chrysler's K platform went into production with the Dodge 400, Chrysler LeBaron, Plymouth Reliant and Dodge Aries. These cars were all front-wheel-drive vehicles with fuel-efficient engines and modern conveniences such as radio-cassette players (and, by the mid-1980s, CD players), central locking, electric windows, electric-window demisters and options that included power seats, electric sunroofs and antilock brakes.

But the component sharing didn't stop at the domestic market. GM's J platform became the basis for the Opel Ascona in Europe, the Vauxhall Cavalier in Britain, the Isuzu Aska in Japan, the Holden Camira in Australia and the Chevrolet Monza in Brazil. Chrysler's K platform was further used as the basis for the Dodge Caravan MPV (Multi Purpose Vehicle). The company had been looking at the MPV minivan concept for several years, with British designer Fergus Pollock creating design studies for Chrysler Europe. These early ideas were lost when Chrysler Europe, which included the British Rootes Group, French car maker Simca and Spanish truck manufacturer Barreiros, was sold to Peugeot in 1978. French engineering company Matra, which had been closely associated with Simca, then acquired the minivan designs. Matra subsequently worked with Renault to produce the Renault Espace MPV in 1984.

Ford Escort

The Mark I Ford Escort was introduced in the United Kingdom at the end of 1967, making its show debut at Brussels Motor Show in January 1968. It replaced the successful long running Anglia. The car was presented in continental Europe as a product of Ford's European operation.

This 1982 American advert for the MKI Ford Escort boasts that it is the only American-built compact with four wheel independent suspension and four doors. The Escort's CVH engine (Compound Valve Hemispherical) is designed to keep scheduled maintenance low due to self-adjusting tappets and electronic ignition. This advert positions the Ford Escort as the perfect family car.

ANNOUNCING FORD ESCORT FOUR-DOOR.

A brand-new World Car.

Since its introduction, Ford Escort has outsold every import car line.* High-technology engineering has given Escort the room and fuel economy to compare with any of the most modern cars, foreign or domestic.

And for 1982, Escort announces four doors for families, four doors for business, four doors for anyone who prefers the extra convenience. And these four doors open up to all the good things that come in an Escort.

*Based on most recent manufacturers' reported retail deliveries.

LOO HERE

t's excellent efficiency.

7 EST HWY **31** EPA EST MPG

...mparison. ...cable only ...dans ...ut power ...ng or AC. ...mileage ...differ de- ...ng on ...d, distance ...weather. ...tual hwy. ...ge lower. Not ...ble in Calif.

World-class engineering, front-wheel drive and more.

Escort is the only American-built compact with four-wheel independent suspension.‡ A front stabilizer bar and all-season radials are standard, too. And you can choose the optional split-torque automatic transmission.

Escort: the driving is easy.

You drive an Escort in a carefully engineered position. Many controls are stalk-mounted for easy access. And the wide selection of options can make Escort's interior as personal as it is convenient.

Everything in its place, comfortably.

Escort is designed with the help of computers to fit one engine, one chassis, a lot of interior appointments and four people quite comfortably into one surprisingly efficient space.

At the heart of the new World Car, the CVH engine.

Escort's CVH engine (Compound Valve Hemispherical) is designed to live on the road, not in the shop.

Because items like self-adjusting tappets and electronic ignition help keep scheduled maintenance low.

Escort hatchback: open up to endless possibilities.

Open Escort four-door's big hatchback and you're looking at over 16 cubic feet of cargo capacity. With the rear seat down you have over 25 cubic feet of cargo room.†

Escort 2-Door Hatchback, Escort 4-Door Wagon and now Escort 4-Door Hatchback. It's a complete line. So choose the Escort that does your kind of commuting, carrying, opening, storing and closing. Whether you buy or lease, see Escort at your Ford Dealer now.

FORD ESCORT

FORD DIVISION (Ford)

‡Excludes other Ford Motor Company products.

†Based on EPA Cargo Volume Index.

K OUT WORLD. ...OMES FORD.

The Espace was not the first MPV to hit the market, with the Toyota Space Cruiser and Nissan Prairie both appearing in 1982, but neither the Japanese nor the French vehicles enjoyed such an enthusiastic public reception as the Dodge Caravan. The minivan idea caught on quickly in America – suddenly a large family outing did not require two or three cars with two or three drivers. The whole family could travel together in comfort.

The major manufacturers not only rationalized production techniques in the 1980s, they began remoulding the entire industry around the world with a series of takeovers and buyouts that saw some previously fiercely independent names that had fallen on hard times being gobbled up. Jaguar extricated itself from the nationalized British Leyland and subsequent Jaguar/Rover/Triumph groups in 1984 and was bought by Ford five years later, only to be sold to India's Tata Motors in 2008. Land Rover, as part of the British Rover Group, was bought by BMW (whose first car was a licence-built British Austin Seven in 1927) who subsequently sold Land Rover to Ford in 2000, Ford then selling it to Tata along with Jaguar.

Ford also bought Aston Martin in 1994, but sold the sports car maker to private investors in 2007, and purchased Volvo in 1999, divesting itself of the Swedish manufacturer in 2010 to Chinese car makers Geely Automobile. Ford's multi-billion-dollar acquisitions of European car makers eventually turned sour when they faced increasing financial difficulties of their own, as did GM who bought SAAB and were forced to sell it 10 years later to Dutch company Spyker Cars. BMW fared somewhat better with their 1998 purchase of Rolls-Royce. The company that began producing the most basic of British cars now manufactures the most prestigious British marque of all. Similarly, Volks-wagen, once rescued from oblivion by the British Army, repaid its debt to British motoring by buying Bentley in 1998 and keeping the famous name alive. The Volkswagen group also includes Audi, Skoda, SEAT, Bugatti and Lamborghini.

As some of the older names in motoring struggled or faded from the scene, bright new stars were rising in the east. Japanese car companies have expanded all over the world, Mazda having enjoyed a partnership with Ford since 1979. The Ford Probe ultimately became a real car in 1989 – a sports coupé – when manufactured alongside the Mazda MX-6 at an assembly facility in Flat Rock, Michigan, now known as the Ford-Mazda AutoAlliance International plant. Nissan, Toyota and Honda all build cars at factories worldwide, including in Britain, and the Koreans have quickly developed into global manufacturers, too.

Kia is South Korea's oldest car company, having been around since 1944. It has been exporting to Europe since 1991, and manufacturing in the USA since 2009, although it is now part of the Hyundai corporation. Hyundai was established in 1967 and now operates the world's largest car plant in Ulsa, South Korea, while also building cars in other countries around the world, from the United States and the Czech Republic to India and China where the Beijing Automotive Company builds not only Hyundai cars but also Mercedes-Benz.

Daewoo is another Korean manufacturer, basically GM's Korean arm, with five plants in the country building vehicles and parts for Chevrolet, Buick, Opel, Vauxhall, Holden and Suzuki.

The motor industry has now gone truly global with more than 50 different countries manufacturing a total in excess of 60 million vehicles. Almost a quarter of those are made by the world's largest vehicle manufacturer, in the People's Republic of China, and the vast majority of those vehicles are for the home market. By 2020 it is estimated that there will be 200 million vehicles in China. It would seem that the Chinese love their cars even more than the Americans do.

LEFT Japanese car maker Honda had developed cars in the 1980s along with British manufacturer Rover, but by 2009 Rover had ceased to be a major player and Honda was successfully building cars in Britain.

The Formula 1 Phenomenon

The FIA Formula 1 World Championship is a competition over a series of Grand Prix races staged at circuits worldwide and featuring the fastest, most advanced, single-seat racing cars in the world. FIA (Fédération Internationale de l'Automobile) is the sport's governing body, based in Paris – almost 120 years after the first motor race, the French are still in charge.

Only the most skilful and talented drivers can hope to maintain control of a Formula 1 car at racing speeds. The cars can reach 354 kmph (220 mph) and corner at speeds high enough to induce a force of up to 5 g. That means the driver will feel a sideways push equivalent to roughly five times his own weight. To put this into perspective, fighter pilots during the Second World War could experience blackouts when pulling between 4 g and 6 g as the force drained blood from their brains, although they had to endure the effect for longer during their high-g manoeuvres than a Formula 1 driver does in cornering.

A Formula 1 car is packed with electronics that allow the driver's support team back in the pits to monitor every aspect of the car's performance. Quite how many performance-enhancing gadgets the engineers can add to a Formula 1 car is controlled by an extensive list of rules and regulations – these are, essentially, the "Formula". As technology has advanced over the years, the Formula rules have expanded to keep pace with the change, although in the beginning, the Formula was really quite simple.

Formula 1 began in 1946 when motor sport started to get back on its wheels in the wake of the Second World War. The events were open to single-seat racing cars with an engine capacity of 4.5 litres, 3 litres for supercharged cars. In fact, 1.5-litre supercharged cars were also permitted because so few of the larger supercharged

This superbly detailed cutaway shows the BRM P57 Formula 1 car in which Graham Hill became World Champion in 1962. The drawing was penned by Brian Hatton who studied at the Beckenham School of Art before joining the staff of *The Motor* in 1954. He produced a wealth of drawings for *The Motor*, becoming head of the magazine's art department and studio manager when *The Motor* merged with The Autocar in 1974. Manufacturers often gave Hatton free access to study not only racing cars but production cars in factory settings in order to produce his artwork. This is not something that could be expected in the motor industry nowadays when the tiniest of technical developments are jealously guarded secrets – especially in the cut-throat world of Formula 1.

OPPOSITE Giuseppe Farina in his Alfa Romeo Tipo 158 on his way to victory in the first of the new Formula 1 races at Silverstone in 1950. He was to become the first Formula 1 World Champion.

OVERLEAF Scotsman Jackie Stewart powers his BRM across the starting line at Silverstone in 1965, the distinctive tartan band around his crash helmet clearly visible. He was to become one of Formula 1's greatest drivers, winning the championship outright three times and holding the record for most race wins (27) for 14 years.

cars still existed. The cars were essentially pre-war models like the Alfa Romeo 158 and Maserati 4CL, making the new Formula 1 an extension of 1930s Grand Prix racing, with drivers like Giuseppe Farina (see page 81), Luigi Villoresi (1909–1997) and Tazio Nuvolari (1892–1953) instantly recognizable from before the war (see pages 42–59, 80–81, 86–87). Races were staged across Europe, but not in Germany, where the country was still recovering from the ravages of war, or in Britain, where there were no suitable venues. To establish Formula 1 so soon after the war was an achievement, but there was no great reward for the drivers at the end of the season. In 1947 it was decided that there should be a Formula 1 Drivers' World Championship and this was instigated in 1950, with the first race staged in Britain on a converted RAF bomber base called Silverstone.

Farina won the 1950 Silverstone race in his Alfa 158 and went on to win the World Championship with his Alfa Romeo team-mates Juan Manuel Fangio (see pages 80–81) and Luigi Fagioli (1898–1952) hot on his heels. It had been a fiercely contested series, especially between Alfa Romeo drivers, but there was

other competition, too. Louis Rosier (1905–1956) chased the Alfas hard in his Talbot-Lago 26C to take fourth place in the championship, Ferrari were making an impact with their 125C and Maserati were still competitive with the 4CLT. All the cars of this period, even when the advanced Mercedes W196 arrived on the scene in 1954, were front-engined, rear-wheel-drive racers with the driver sitting quite high in the cockpit as the drive shaft connecting the engine to the rear wheels had to pass underneath him. In 1957, the Cooper T43 showed a real glimpse of the future when Jack Brabham (see page 86) raced it at the Monaco Grand Prix. The car had the engine mounted behind the driver, but in front of the rear wheels. This gave far better weight distribution, allowing the driver to sit lower within the car's bodywork, reducing the frontal area and improving streamlining. Stirling Moss (see box feature page 83) drove a T34 to victory in the 1958 Argentine Grand Prix, making it the first rear-engined car to win a Formula 1 World Championship event, and in 1959 Jack Brabham became World Champion driving the T34's successor, the T45.

ABOVE Ayrton Senna leads his McLaren team-mate Alain Prost during the San Marino Grand Prix at Imola in 1989. Despite driving for the same team, the two were bitter rivals. On this occasion, Senna finished first and Prost second.

OPPOSITE Sebastian Vettel on his way to winning the Abu Dhabi Grand Prix in 2010 and becoming the youngest-ever World Champion at the age of just 23.

OVERLEAF The pit crew swarms around Lewis Hamilton's McLaren-Mercedes during the Chinese Grand Prix in 2009. From 2010, refuelling was no longer permitted, cars having to start the race with sufficient fuel, so the emphasis was on changing the wheels, the pit-stop target time being less than 3.5 seconds!

Ayrton Senna (1960–1994)

Voted by Formula 1 drivers in at least two separate media polls as the greatest Formula 1 driver of all time, Ayrton Senna da Silva won 41 Formula 1 races out of 161 starts, becoming World Champion in 1988, 1990 and 1991. Born in Sao Paulo, Brazil, Senna's father was wealthy enough to indulge his son's passion for motorsport, which he began with go-kart racing. At the age of 13, Senna won the South American Kart Championship, and in 1981 he moved to the UK to begin his progression through Formula Ford and Formula 3 to Formula 1. In 1984 he made his Formula 1 debut with the Toleman team at the Brazilian Grand Prix in Rio. Senna drove for Lotus in 1985, moving to McLaren in 1988 and on to Williams in 1994. He died in a high-speed crash while leading the San Marino Grand Prix at Imola. The Brazilian government declared three days of mourning and his funeral procession in Sao Paulo was witnessed by around three million people.

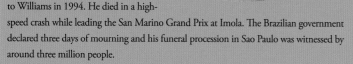

From then on, rear-engined cars dominated Formula 1 and in 1968 the Lotus 49B was raced with a rear "wing" mounted on struts high above the car. The wing gave the car "downforce" that helped it to grip the track and over the next few years Formula 1 cars sprouted all sorts of aerodynamic wings and spoilers until it was estimated that, above a certain speed, the pressure pushing the wheels onto the driving surface was enough for a Formula 1 car to drive on the ceiling – given a big enough ceiling. The Lotus 49B was also notable in that it introduced a tobacco sponsor's livery to a Formula 1 car for the first time. The red-white-gold Gold Leaf Team Lotus colours gave way to the black-and-gold of the John Player Special Lotus in 1971, although the gold was actually more of a beige colour. This was to make it look like gold when the car was seen on TV.

Television, sponsorship, merchandise and big business have grown to dominate Formula 1, with an estimated total in excess of 527 million viewers worldwide having followed the races in the 2010 season. That season consisted of 19 races, starting in Bahrain and roving around the world through Australia, Malaysia and China to India, Abu Dhabi and Brazil. The entire sport is a multi-billion-dollar enterprise and the drivers are the world's finest. They begin as children racing in kart contests, then move on through the lower "formulas" such as Formula BMW and Formula Three, with the cars becoming ever faster and more sophisticated. The stress on modern drivers is enormous and they have to be supremely fit, making modern Grand Prix racing something of a young man's game. Sebastian Vettel was just 23 years old when he won the Drivers' Championship in 2010, winning five of the 19 races and finishing on the podium a total of 10 times. When Giuseppe Farina became champion 60 years earlier, he was 43 and needed to win just three out of six events that were all staged in Europe with no other podium finishes.

The Car Goes Green

In London in 1952, what became known as "The Great Smog" filled the air, reducing daytime sunlight over 4 to 9 December to little more than a glimmer. The smog (an amalgamation of the words "smoke" and "fog") was caused by smoke from coal fires, coal-fired power stations, industrial emissions and vehicle exhaust fumes. The majority of homes around the capital were heated with open coal fires and the cold weather had meant that people were burning more coal than usual. The cloud of smog that enveloped Britain's capital city caused respiratory problems for countless people, leading to the premature deaths of at least 4,000.

RIGHT This 1974 CitiCar was built in Florida, had plastic body panels to save weight and could carry two people over a distance of around 80 km (50 miles) at up to 45 kmph (28 mph). It was intended to help solve the 1970s fuel crisis and was inspired by a golf-cart design.

While smog was not a new phenomenon in London and other large cities, it was now becoming clear that the car and other motor vehicles were contributing heavily to the problem. In Los Angeles, a slightly different kind of smog was identified in the 1950s – photochemical smog. This happened when emissions from industrial plants, power stations and motor vehicles reacted in the atmosphere with strong sunlight to produce a blanket of toxic chemical particles that hovered over the city. The Californian Air Resources Board found that more than 50 per cent of this smog was caused by vehicle emissions.

Kiichiro Toyoda (1894–1952)

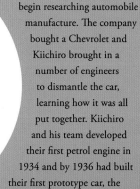

The founder of the Toyota Motor Corporation, Kiichiro Toyoda was born in Aichi Prefecture in Japan, the son of industrialist Sakichi Toyoda, who made a fortune manufacturing innovative weaving looms for the textile industry. Kiichiro studied engineering at the University of Tokyo and travelled to Britain and the United States to learn about industrial manufacturing. In the early 1930s, he was given the backing of Toyoda Industries to begin researching automobile manufacture. The company bought a Chevrolet and Kiichiro brought in a number of engineers to dismantle the car, learning how it was all put together. Kiichiro and his team developed their first petrol engine in 1934 and by 1936 had built their first prototype car, the A1. It used parts copied from Ford and the styling was strongly reminiscent of the Chrysler Airflow. The name "Toyoda" is associated with farming, so the new, slightly altered company name "Toyota Motor Company" was registered in 1937. Kiichiro remained involved with the company until 1950 when he resigned, with the company floundering during Japan's post-war recession. His cousin, Eiji Toyoda (1913–2013), took over and oversaw the gradual expansion of the company.

The health risks led to cities around the world cleaning up their acts, introducing smokeless zones and taking steps to control the emissions from factories and power stations. Clearly, the next problem to be tackled was the car. In the mid-1950s, French engineer Eugene Houdry (1892–1962), who lived in America, developed the catalytic converter. This was a kind of exhaust filter that used reactive chemicals to convert harmful exhaust gases, such as carbon monoxide, to less harmful substances like carbon dioxide. But it was to be another 20 years before the catalytic converter was in widespread use because petrol contained an additive called tetra-ethyl lead. This had been introduced to petrol in the 1920s to help prevent the fuel from pre-igniting in the combustion chamber, and in doing so it improved the performance and power output of the engine. Exhaust gases containing lead compounds, however, coated the surface of the catalytic converter's filters, rendering them useless. Lead is, of course, a powerful pollutant and when legislation was introduced by governments around the world in the mid-1970s to eliminate lead compounds from exhaust gases, unleaded petrol became available and the catalytic converter came into its own.

The car was, therefore, already cleaning up its act when the ecological movement began to gather pace, with concerns about pollution heightened by the reported effects of global warming. The car was identified as a major culprit and manufacturers began competing to see who could produce the most fuel-efficient, least polluting, "greenest" cars. Diesel engines, which burn fuel more efficiently than petrol engines, became an increasingly popular option and by the 1990s diesel engines were available in all sorts of cars from the lowliest Fiat Uno to the grandest Mercedes S-Class. Cadillac began experimenting with diesel in 1978 and also had a V-8 engine that would shut down some of its cylinders when less power was required, conserving fuel and thus lowering emissions. Neither of these Cadillac innovations were a success at the time, suffering from reliability teething problems, but they serve to show that even America's premier car brand was starting to try to think green.

Even with computer-controlled electronic engine management systems, the most frugal petrol or diesel engines cannot avoid venting exhaust gas to the atmosphere, so they will never be able to achieve the ultimate environmental goal of zero emissions. The only way to have zero emissions is to forgo using an engine that burns fossil fuels – the electric car was the obvious solution. Although electric passenger cars went out of fashion in the 1920s (see pages 19, 26, 31), Smith Electric Vehicles in England continued to produce electric delivery vehicles, notably the ubiquitous "milk float", and joined forces with American battery producer Exide and coachbuilder Boyertown to make electric delivery trucks for America in the 1960s. In 1974 the US Postal Service, which had a tradition of electric-vehicle use stretching back to 1899, ordered 350 electric trucks from AMC, including 40 electric Jeeps. The Postal Service continues to use a variety of electric vehicles to this day. Electric power on the highway, therefore, had never quite disappeared, but the old problems of limited range and long recharging periods meant that it remained out of favour as the power behind the car.

ABOVE Toyota has become one of the world's leading proponents of hybrid technology, having sold around 3 million vehicles worldwide. Their "plug-in" hybrid has an extra set of batteries that are charged directly from a mains electricity outlet. The car automatically switches to its onboard petrol/electric system when the "plug-in" power is exhausted.

RIGHT SUVs like the GMC Yukon have been easy targets for green campaigners as these heavy vehicles use large, thirsty engines, but even these cars now have hybrid versions that are more environmentally friendly.

The "green" movement was to change that. Experimental electric town cars such as Sebring-Vanguard's CitiCar began appearing in the Seventies. More than 2,000 Citicars were produced from 1974 to 1977, based largely on golf-cart technology, with roughly the same number of its successor Comuta-Car and Comuta-Van models built up to 1982. These cars were quite crude, however, when compared to GM's EV1 in 1996. Based on a 1990 concept car, the EV1 was leased to customers in Los Angeles, Phoenix and Tucson as a kind of extended trial. A year after the EV1 went into production, Toyota launched the Prius Hybrid in Japan. Instead of having an electric motor that needed to be charged overnight and then provided only limited driving range the next day, the Prius had a small but efficient petrol engine as well as an electric motor. The car could be started and driven as an electric vehicle, providing quiet and pollution-free motoring in town, but the engine would kick in to recharge the battery when it was running low, or when more power was needed for out-of-town driving. It was an idea that appealed to the public, although the cost of providing an internal combustion engine as well as the latest electric technology meant that the Prius was initially sold at a loss by Toyota, otherwise it would have seemed exceedingly expensive alongside conventional family-car rivals. Toyota extended the hybrid concept over the next few years to cover certain models across their range of vehicles right up to the luxury Lexus models. By the end of 2010 they had sold more than 1 million hybrids in Japan and almost 3 million worldwide.

The Hybrid concept was adopted in a variety of forms by almost every other manufacturer. Even gas-guzzling SUVs (Sports Utility Vehicles) like the GMC Yukon, with its 6-litre V-8 engine, spawned hybrid versions, as did the top-of-the-range BMW 7 series luxury saloon, although the Hybrid 7 was not a full hybrid, since an electric motor provided assistance to the 4.4-litre petrol engine for optimum performance and fuel efficiency rather than the car driving on electric power alone.

Yet there was still room in the modern, ecologically sound world for outrageous supercars. In 2008, Tesla Motors of California, with a little help from Lotus, produced the Tesla Roadster. It had classic supercar looks and could accelerate through 0–97 kmph (0–60 mph) in 3.9 seconds, yet it was also the first all-electric car with battery technology that gave it a range in excess of 322 km (200 miles). And at the Geneva Motor Show in 2011, Porsche launched its Panamera hybrid sports car while Mercedes-Benz showed the all-electric version of the SLS AMG with four electric motors, one for each wheel – a bit like Ferdinand Porshe's Mixte Hybrid 110 years earlier (see pages 26–27, 31).

Retro Styling

What happens when kids brought up in the 1960s watching films on TV that were made 10 years earlier grow up to find themselves in charge of major manufacturers' car design studios? The answer is that they indulge their childhood dreams and experiment with styling that has always appealed to them as aesthetically pleasing, well proportioned, graceful, beautiful… or just cool. Designer Frank Stephenson (see box feature), who was responsible for the new MINI for BMW in 2001 (see below) and the Fiat 500 in 2007, has described how he felt that car design had lost its way and cars no longer had flowing, sensual lines or the kind of shapes that made you want to run your hand along the bodywork. They might be designed using computers, but did cars really have to have the sharp edges and angles that made them look as if they had been designed *by* computers?

BELOW Longer, wider and taller than the 1959 version, Frank Stephenson's 2001 MINI for BMW was built in Britain and, just like the original, hit a production volume of one million cars in its first six years.

Stephenson certainly wasn't alone in looking to the past for inspiration. A 1940s-style hot-rod design produced by Chip Foose (1963–) while he was at the Art Center College of Design in Pasadena, California (where Stephenson also studied) served as the basis for the Plymouth Prowler in 1979. The low-slung dragster with open, cycle-type front mudguards saw very limited production when first introduced, but would go on to sell almost 12,000, with the most expensive variants costing up to US$45,000. Customers were not only paying for the style, and they certainly were not paying for luxury, but the Prowler did provide acceleration to match its dragster looks, hitting 97 kmph (60 mph) from a standing start in under 6 seconds.

Another Pasadena Art Center graduate, J Mays (1954–), designed a car that was to have a far greater production run than the Prowler, the 1998 Volkswagen New Beetle. Although it was not to have the phenomenal production life of its much-loved predecessor, the New Beetle was an instant hit all over the world. Any fans of

the original Beetle lifting the boot lid to examine the engine were in for something of a shock because the New Beetle was not a rear-engined, rear-wheel-drive car like its ancestor. Instead, it had its engine in the front, driving the front wheels. The curvaceous wings and rounded shape, however, left no one in any doubt about the New Beetle's heritage.

Jaguar had always liked to employ a continuity of styling that maintained proud links with its past. Until the all-new XJ saloon was introduced in 2009, Jaguar's flagship executive car retained a distinct family resemblance to previous models, but it was with the 1999 S-type that retro styling really came into play. The oval grille, round headlights and roof line that curved into a rounded rear end all paid tribute to the original S-Type of 1963, but this new Jaguar, despite having been created by the company's British design director Geoff Lawson (1944–1999), had a strong American influence. Jaguar was then owned by Ford and the S-Type used the same platform as Ford's Lincoln LS and the 2002 Ford Thunderbird. This eleventh-generation Thunderbird was also the subject of a retro-styling exercise, again by J Mays, although it turned out looking rather more like the original 1955 Thunderbird's rival, the Chevrolet Corvette, than it did the Ford.

Yet another American retro-mobile from the beginning of the twenty-first century was the Chrysler PT Cruiser. With styling prompts harking all the way back to the Chrysler Airflow of 1934 (see pages 49), the PT Cruiser had the look of a custom car and epitomized the retro design ethos with a real spirit of fun. Designed by Bryan

ABOVE Roberto Giolito was the designer responsible for the new Fiat 500, his 2007 version bearing a very close family resemblance to the 1957 original but including significant differences, such as the engine being at the front, driving the front wheels, instead of at the back driving the rear ones.

Frank Stephenson (1959–)

Frank Stephenson has always enjoyed a cosmopolitan lifestyle, having been born in Casablanca, Morocco, where he lived with his Norwegian father and Spanish mother until he was 11 years old. He then moved to Istanbul in Turkey for five years before attending high school in Madrid in Spain. After a few years racing in motocross, he attended the famous Art Center College of Design in Pasadena, California and by the age of 26 he was working in Ford's design department in Cologne in Germany. Munich was his next stop, where he worked for BMW on the X5 and made his mark as the designer of the new MINI. Stephenson spent 11 years at BMW before becoming design director at Ferrari and Maserati in 2002. Three years later, he was design director for the Fiat Group, producing – among other iconic cars – the retro-styled Fiat 500. Stephenson moved to England in 2008 to join McLaren Automotive in Surrey, working on their next generation of supercars.

PREVIOUS PAGES Designed by Jaguar's director of styling, Geoff Lawson, the 1999 S-Type saloon took its styling cues from Jaguar's 1963 S-Type, although the 1999 car actually shared many component parts with Ford's Lincoln LS, Ford having bought Jaguar in 1989.

ABOVE The Chrysler PT Cruiser of 1999 had a hint of the 1934 Airflow in its looks but it was considerably more successful, selling 1.35 million over its 10-year production run.

OPPOSITE The design of the Ferrari 612 Scaglietti was inspired by the styling of the 1954 "Ingrid Bergman" Ferrari 375 but it is much faster than its predecessor. With a top speed of 315 kmph (196 mph), it can accelerate to 97 kmph (60 mph) from a standing start in a little over 4 seconds.

Nesbitt (1969–), another graduate from Pasadena's Art Center College, the PT Cruiser was available as a five-door hatchback or two-door convertible, remaining in production from 2000 until 2010 and selling 1.35 million vehicles around the world.

Frank Stephenson's new MINI (spelt out in capitals to distinguish it from the original 1959 Mini) was several years in the making prior to its launch in 2001. The styling, of course, was reminiscent of Issigonis's masterpiece (see page 78–79), although the lumps and bumps had been smoothed out, but this was not the basic, inexpensive city car of 1959. The new MINI was fully loaded with computer hardware providing electronic throttle control, electronic brake force distribution, electronic stability control and cornering brake control. Underneath their quaint styling, retro cars were thoroughly modern machines.

Other Stephenson retro projects included the Ferrari 612 Scaglietti of 2004, designed by Pininfarina under Stephenson's watchful eye as an homage to the "Ingrid Bergman" Ferrari 375 of 1954 (see page 70–71). He also supervised the Fiat 500, launched in 2007, 50 years after the original. Based on a concept created by Fiat designer Roberto

Giolito in 2004, the new Fiat 500 was brought to life with Stephenson in charge of Fiat's styling. Around one-third cheaper than the rival MINI, just as its predecessor was cheaper than the old Mini, the 500 was based on the same platform as Ford's Ka.

The evidence would appear to point to a strong American driving force behind the retro movement and there were certainly plenty of examples speeding out of American design studios. In 2004, Ford produced the GT, a striking rendition of the GT40 which won at Le Mans four years in succession from 1966 to 1969. Chrysler introduced the 300C in 2005, a car with the same sort of menacing poise as the old C300 of 1955; Dodge produced a 2008 version of their 1970 Challenger muscle car; and, in 2010, Chevrolet revealed their new retro Camaro.

The ultimate retro design, however, has to be the fabulous Mercedes-Benz SLS AMG with its side-vent louvres, rounded tail and gull-wing doors giving the supercar classic looks to enhance its breathtaking performance – 0–97 kmph (0–60 mph) in only 3.8 seconds and a top speed electronically limited to 317 kmph (197 mph). For kids brought up in the 1960s, that's a real dream car.

Into the Future

There was a time when you could let everyone know how well you were doing by making sure you were seen driving a car as big as an ocean liner with an engine that rumbled like thunder. Your neighbours, the guy sitting in the car next to you at the traffic lights and especially the geek on the moped at the filling station would know that you could afford to spend a fortune running a very expensive car. It's still possible to do that today. You can buy a car that drinks fuel as if it's going out of fashion – but it really is going out of fashion. Everyone knows that oil is going to run out one day, although nobody's quite certain exactly when, and that burning fossil fuels is, in any case, affecting the environment. To attract admiring glances nowadays, what you really need to be seen in is a car that's kind to the planet. And in the future, ecologically sound motoring will be an aim that we all take for granted.

There are now almost 3.5 million hybrid electric vehicles on the road around the world, technology that many now see as the mainstream alternative to pure petrol or diesel cars, but these hybrids are a mere stepping stone on the way to a petrol-free future. There are already three times as many vehicles around the world that run on natural gas than there are petrol/electric hybrids, and all of the major motor manufacturers have produced cars that will run on CNG (Compressed Natural Gas). But natural gas is burned in an internal combustion engine and, although it may be "cleaner" than petrol or diesel, it is still a fossil fuel and, like oil, will run out eventually.

There are twice as many flexible-fuel vehicles as there are vehicles running on natural gas. Flexible-fuel cars have engines that can burn more than one type of fuel, such as ethanol or hydrogen. Ethanol is an old favourite of the motor car

and early cars like the Model T Ford (see pages 14–19) were capable of running on ethanol as well as petrol. Ethanol is the same kind of alcohol that is found in common drinking spirits like vodka or whisky and it can be made from agricultural crops including grain, potatoes or sugar cane. While it would appear that this makes ethanol a truly renewable energy source, it does nonetheless pollute the atmosphere when burned in an engine, and to produce enough of it to replace petrol, vast swathes of fertile farmland much needed for food production would have to be dedicated to growing crops for ethanol. The same is true of most "bio-fuels" derived from farmed crops. Hydrogen, on the other hand, burns cleanly. Nothing burns without oxygen, as burning is a chemical process whereby a substance combines with oxygen. When hydrogen combines with oxygen, it produces water. Unfortunately, making hydrogen is an energy-intensive process,

LEFT The new Ford Evos lightweight electric concept car. As well as having impeccable green credentials this car interacts with the driver, adapting handling, steering and other controls to suit the individual. It even claims to monitor the driver's physical state and adjusts the driving experience accordingly.

OPPOSITE Guy Negre of Motor Development International with his Air Pod creations, cars that have engines that run on compressed air and are steered using a joystick – much like the very first cars featured in this book!

OVERLEAF The BMW i8, the new concept electric sports car which was showcased at the Autumn 2011 International Automobile Ausstellung (IAA).

but it may be possible to produce it in an environmentally sound manner in the not-too-distant future, perhaps by using naturally generated electricity in the electrolysis of water – separating hydrogen from oxygen in water. When the hydrogen is then burned as a fuel, you go back to having water again.

Hydrogen can also be used in a fuel cell, which produces electricity in much the same way that a battery does, relying on the reaction between two chemicals to produce a flow of electrons – an electric current. The big difference between a battery and a fuel cell is that a battery stores a set amount of each chemical that is used up during the reaction while in a fuel cell the chemicals can be "topped up" to keep the reaction going. Topping up the hydrogen and allowing it to react with oxygen from the air to produce electricity could be a way of powering future electric vehicles, and several major manufacturers already have cars – the GM Sequel and Honda FCX Clarity are two examples – in limited production to evaluate the hydrogen fuel cell's viability.

But why use fuel at all when you can run an engine on pure air? Actually, you need compressed air that could be fed into the cylinder of an engine, expanding to drive the cylinder in the same way that a steam engine works. Compressed air clearly produces no pollutants when it runs an engine, although a great deal of energy is required to compress the air in the first place. Indian manufacturer Tata have been exploring the possibilities of compressed-air engines, as have Honda and a number of other companies, although there are problems with limited range, refuelling and the air cooling as it expands.

In the future we will also see new technology used to conserve or reuse energy within the car itself. Electric vehicles are already starting to use regenerative braking, whereby the wheels of a car with an electric motor are slowed by the motor going into reverse. In reverse, the motor actually becomes a generator and tops up the car's batteries. This system is used on a number of vehicles including the Porsche Panamera Hybrid. BMW are even using the waste heat from the engine in their Turbosteamer to bring steam power back into fashion. The system uses the hot exhaust to turn water into steam that is then fed into a steam piston which helps to drive the crankshaft.

Future cars will be packed with the very latest technology and there will be different cars, probably running on different fuels, to suit different motoring needs. One view of a new city car comes from the Massachusetts Institute of Technology (MIT), which has been considering reinventing the way we use the car completely. Their "MIT" car would be a shared vehicle that you could pick up from a street kiosk where they would stack like shopping trolleys. Flip it open, jump in and off you go, leaving the car at a convenient kiosk near your destination for the next driver who needs it.

Driver? What driver? Some people believe that future cars won't need a driver at all – well, not all the time, anyway. The driver will be able to sit back and relax while an automated highway system takes over. This might be an intelligent road that talks to your car's computer so that they can work out between them the best way to get you to your destination, or it might take the form of car "platoons" with cars talking to each other. The leading vehicle in a car platoon would take control of a string of following vehicles, this lead vehicle ensuring that the others operated at peak efficiency. The cars' computers would work together to maintain safe distances and make good progress while the drivers sat back, had a sandwich or took a nap until the cars told them it was time to leave the platoon. The car of the future may not only be easy on the environment but may also take the stress out of motoring. And how cool would it be for you to be seen by your neighbours, that guy at the traffic lights and the geek at the filling station, when you are sitting in a car that does everything for you? You don't need to drive it – it drives you wherever you want to go!

That may not be every driver's idea of a perfect motoring future but it is one possible road that tomorrow's car might take. What the car will look like is anyone's guess, but there will undoubtedly be large cars, small cars, fast cars and family cars – cars to suit the diverse needs of the motoring public. Only one thing is certain: so many different options are under consideration for the car of tomorrow that change is sure to come, just as it always has done ever since Karl Benz patented his original Motorwagen.

Index

Credits

Picture Credits

The publishers would like to thank the following sources for their kind permission to reproduce the pictures in this book.

Alamy Images: /artpartner-images.com: 154, /B Christopher: 112-113, /Martyn Goddard: 111t, /Interfoto: 67tl, /Mary Evans Picture Library: 6, /Mirrorpix: 62t, /Motoring Picture Library: 148, /philipus: 156-157, /Photos 12: 105br, /Phil Talbot: 70, /Transtock: 76, 94, 96, 153, /Tom Wood: 5, 121b

Alfa Romeo Automobilismo Storico: /Centro Documentazione (Arese,Milano): 77b

Bridgeman Images: /DaTo Images: 75; Peter Newark American Pictures: 74, /Roger Perrin: 84tl

Bugatti Automobiles: 31b

Corbis: 11tr, 17tr, 40, 141, /Bettmann: 8b, 8t, 10bl, 10br, 12t, 19b, 31tr, 32, 80, 145, /Car Culture: 27, 63, 64-65, 90, 118, /epa: 129, 149, /Martyn Goddard: 52-53, 89, 108b, 150-151, /Don Heiny: 79, /Hulton-Deutsch Collection: 19tr, 36, /Schlegelmilch: 140bl, 142-143, /Tony Korody/Sygma: 97br, /JP Laffont/Sygma: 112tl, /Jeffrey Markowitz/Sygma: 110, /Jean-Yves Ruszniewski/TempSport: 140t, /Universal/TempSport: 84-85, /Transtock: 19tc, 72-73, 77t, 97t, 98-99, 115, 116-117, 130, 152, /Underwood & Underwood: 71bl

Daimler Chrysler: 24, 47b, 55

Donington Park Collection: 86tl, 86tr, 87

General Motors: 146-147

Getty Images: 14, 16-17, 21tl, 33, 37t, 38-39, 59tr, 59b, 66, 78br, 83t, 83br, 125br, 136, 144, /AFP: 88, 128b, 131tr, 134-135, 155, /Bloomberg: 146tl, /Car Culture: 91, 100, 119br, /Gamma-Keystone: 121tl, /Martyn Goddard: 114, /ISC Archives: 44t, /Imagno: 54r, / Klemantaski Collection: 138-139, /National Motor Museum/Heritage Images: 29, /Popperfoto: 43, 120, /Science & Society Picture Library: 7, 18, 21tr, 48-49, 54b, /Otto Stadler: 65br, /Time & Life Pictures: 81, /Underwood Archives: 102-103; /Roger Viollet: 12b

Haymarket Consumer Media: /Brain Hatton & Dick Ellis cut-away drawings: 119t, 137

JDHT: /Jaguar Heritage: 82

LAT Photographic: 47tr, 124, 125t, 126-127, 128tl

Lamborghini: 95tr

Mary Evans Picture Library: 21b, 41, 78t, /The Institution of Mechanical Engineers: 22-23, /Museum of the City of New York: 26, /Onslow Auction Limited: 45, /Rue des Archives/ Tallandier: 28, 30, /Rue des Archives/Varma: 51

Mercedes-Benz: 48bl

Motoring Picture Library: 20, 25tr, 25b, 35tr, 35b, 42, 62br, 111b

Press Association Images: /AP: 60-61, /Sutton Motorsport: 44br

Photos 12: /Archives du 7e Art/DR: 104

Picture Desk: /Paramount/Kobal Collection: 108t

Private Collection: 13, 50b, 50tr, 60, 68tl, /american-automobiles.com: 49tr

Rex Features: /Daily Mail/Graham Trott: 131b, /Everett Collection: 101, /Sony Pics/Everett: 105t, /Martyn Goddard: 116tl, /Jonathan Hordle: 109, /Magic Car Pics: 132-133, /National Motor Museum: 106-107, 122-123

Science & Society Picture Library: /Science Museum Archive: 15

Shutterstock.com: 3

Topfoto.co.uk: 34, 46, 58, 67b, 71t, /National Motor Museum/HIP: 37b, 56-57, 92-93, / Ullsteinbild: 9b, 68-69, /World History Archive: 9t

US National Archives: 11b

Volvo: 95b, 131tl

Memorabilia Credits

The publishers would like to thank the following sources for their kind permission to reproduce the documents in this book.

Private Collection: page 11

US National Archives: page 13

Science Museum Archive/Science & Society Picture Library: page 15

The Institution of Mechanical Engineers/Mary Evans Picture Library: page 22–22

Onslow Auction Limited/Mary Evans Picture Library: page 45

Varma/Rue des Archives/Mary Evans Picture Library: page 51

Peter Newark American Pictures/The Bridgeman Art Library: page 74

DaTo Images/The Bridgeman Art Library: page 75

Alfa Romeo Automobilismo Storico, Centro Documentazione (Arese, Milano): page 77

Mary Evans Picture Library: page 78

Jaguar Heritage, © JDHT: page 83 and 119

Roger Perrin/The Bridgeman Art Library: page 84

Donington Park Collection: page 86–87

Brian Hatton and Dick Ellis cut-away drawings, courtesy of Haymarket Consumer Media: page 137

Every effort has been made to acknowledge correctly and contact the source and/or copyright holder of each picture and item of memorabilia and Carlton Books Limited apologises for any unintentional errors or omissions which will be corrected in future editions of this book.